Walk with God
and win
SPIRITUAL
WARFARE

Win the Battle of the Mind
through Prayer Tools for
Spiritual Excellence, Intimacy
with God, and Experiencing
God in Breakthroughs

Mike Tirivacho

Walk with God and Win Spiritual Warfare

ISBN: 978-1-77934-250-8
miketirichoo@gmail.com

CONTENTS

PREFACE

This book aims to ignite a believer's spiritual growth, leading to a strong and fervent spirit that actively seeks divine answers. The most effective way to win spiritual battles is unwavering faith and engaging in a consistent and effective prayer life. Christians should strive to build a connection or relationship with God and engage in prayers that positively impact their daily lives. This practice not only fosters personal transformation, but also enables them to effect positive change in the lives of others while growing spiritually.

Many Christians experience "spiritual dryness" and sadness in their lives. The enemy is at war, seeking to steal the goodness and joy God has granted to individuals. Christians find joy not just in answered prayers but also in overcoming temptations meant to weaken their faith. To overcome these trials of spiritual warfare, believers should seek God's Word for growth and guidance through the empowering presence of the Holy Spirit.

Chapter 5 outlines the essential prayer components necessary for the Body of Christ (the church) to thrive effectively. In today's fast-paced world, the modern church faces unique challenges. How can we ensure its endurance through the end times?

After reading this book, readers should be able to transform their lives and address the following five questions related to faith and spirituality:

1. In what areas does the enemy have a foothold in my life, and how is he continuously suppressing my potential to break free?

2. How can I identify, confront, and bind the enemy's plans so that God delivers me and my family from the demonic forces that have caused pain and suffering in my life, whether in health, relationships, or finances?

3. What steps can I take to strengthen my faith, draw closer to God, and cultivate a deeper desire to spend more time with Him?

4. How can I enhance my prayer life to speak things into existence and combat the schemes of darkness, enabling me to fulfill God's purpose and experience breakthroughs?

5. What steps can I take to improve myself and achieve my full potential and goals, despite setbacks caused by the enemy?

INTRODUCTION

There are times when we worship God with the expectation of receiving things we desire from Him. When the enemy realizes this, he comes with a wind of disruption and resistance, leading to frustration in our hearts when things don't go as we hoped.

The Bible encourages us to "fight the good fight of faith" in 1 Timothy 6:12. This means we must maintain our focus on God and draw near to Him, as this is the best way to win spiritual battles. Concentrating more on our challenges and circumstances instead of God can negatively impact our mental strength and zeal for prayer, especially since life is dynamic and always changing.

This book will provide tips on how to draw near to Jesus in ways that can hinder the enemy's schemes. When it comes to overcoming obstacles in our journey of faith in Jesus, there are four fundamental factors every Christian must consider:

1. A Christian's life and decision-making should be guided by the Holy Spirit.

2. We must always boldly approach the throne of grace to find help in times of need through faith and repentance. When we feel defeated in any area of our lives, we should never "faint," lose hope, or waver in our faith; instead, we should ask for more grace, wisdom, and patience.

3. We must persevere in prayer and declare the power of the blood of Jesus upon our lives and against the forces of darkness, knowing that God has equipped us through Jesus Christ.

4. We should grow spiritually in grace and support one another, bearing each other's burdens. Sometimes, confronting the forces of darkness requires corporate prayer, comforting one another, and helping each other until we all attain perfect unity in faith.

Many Christians continue to live oppressed and fall into the enemy's snares, even after receiving the grace of salvation through repentance. Thus, the Christian faith necessitates believers to use prayer as a weapon of spiritual warfare and gain wisdom to identify the traps the enemy has set in their lives.

Are you facing challenges that overwhelm you physically, financially, or emotionally? Is your family caught in a cycle of relationship issues that cause tension and frustration? If setbacks such as illness, addiction, poverty, or failure seem persistent, it's crucial to recognize that these struggles can indicate deeper, negative spiritual influences at play in your life. As soon as you identify the enemy's schemes or notice something amiss, start confronting the enemy with a prayer of faith concerning your situation. Every Christian should never forsake the weapon of prayer and faith as long as they are on the battleground against the enemy.

The more we grow in faith and engage in prayer, the more we allow the Holy Spirit to take control of our circumstances. He will fight our battles so much that no weapon formed by the enemy can prosper against us. Therefore, when a Christian consistently yields to the Holy Spirit, there is an assurance of joy and victory.

This book also aims to reveal ways to identify the enemy's schemes, helping individuals free themselves from the devil's oppression and strengthen their connection with God. In the first two chapters, the author frequently references Old Testament scriptures to elaborate on spiritual warfare.

CHAPTER I

A THORN IN MY FLESH

AND

HOW TO REMOVE IT

Why Spiritual Warfare: The Purpose of the Battle

Spiritual warfare is the struggle to overcome evil forces that oppose salvation (the gift of eternal life through redemption) and adherence to God's Word in obedience. It entails resisting temptations, standing firm in faith, and engaging in regular prayer to overcome these forces. This battle is not against flesh and blood, but against spiritual entities that aim to lead believers astray. However, we can also embrace a more uplifting view of spiritual warfare by recognizing that every triumph in this battle pleases God and glorifies Him. He eagerly desires our redemption, empowering us to conquer the devil through our unwavering faith. Rest assured, God will uplift His people at the right moment, and transform their lives.

The Implications of Spiritual Warfare

Engaging in any conflict requires a clear understanding of what one is entering into. If unprepared, a person may suffer unnecessary pain, loss of resources, or even life. In spiritual warfare, Christ encourages Christians to remain vigilant and aware of the trials they will encounter. This awareness is crucial to ensure they do not falter when confronted with resistance from the enemy (Luke 9:62; 14:28-32; 8:4-15).

Since his condemnation, the devil has waged a relentless campaign against humanity (Revelation 12:12). He aims to impose the forces of darkness, causing pain and suffering, and drawing people away from obeying God's Word. He introduces obstacles into our paths that haunt us, pressuring us to seek alternative ways of living rather than following God's path. Through deception and temptation, many individuals are led astray, ultimately missing out on the precious gift of salvation that awaits them.

The Struggle Against Idolatry: A Call to Action

A prayer altar is a blessing when it is genuinely directed toward God. However, deceptive altars lead people astray (2 Chronicles 28:24- 25). An altar is any sacred capacity or entity for conducting a reverential and consecrated offering or sacrifice to a higher spiritual authority or power.

True worship is always directed toward God through Jesus Christ. The root of genuine worship is yielding to God with a heart that seeks the gospel through prayer and the sacrifice of fruitful deeds. Diversion of focus from God to worship any other altar, spiritual power, object, or individual—especially as a source of refuge or reverence—is considered idolatry.

It took a long time (40 years) for the children of Israel to occupy the Promised Land. This was because of their disobedience, hardness of heart towards God's covenant, and unbelief (Hebrews 3:7-12). Therefore, if we do not entirely deal with our errors and deviations from God's Word, we will eventually fall short of God's promises and blessings (Hebrews 3:17-19; 4:1-2).

Many obstacles, or idolatrous altars, get in the way of our lives and, at most times, become a snare to our spiritual growth. One of the most pervasive and abhorrent sins throughout the time of the Old Covenant was idolatry.

> *Joshua 7:13 Get up, sanctify the people, and say, 'Sanctify yourselves for tomorrow, because thus says the Lord God of Israel: "There is an accursed thing in your midst, O Israel; you cannot stand before your enemies until you take away the accursed thing from among you."*

In like manner, the LORD urges us to turn away from these "dark altars," or anything that is worshipped, trusted, or cherished in place of God Himself. These things hinder our spiritual progress and oppose God's ways and His Word.

> *2 Corinthians 6:17-18*
>
> *17 Therefore*
>
> *"Come out from among them*
>
> *And be separate, says the Lord.*
>
> *Do not touch what is unclean,*

And I will receive you."

18 'I will be a Father to you,

And you shall be My sons and daughters,

Says the Lord Almighty."

Similarly, we often make worldly agreements and covenants with unbelievers through cultures, traditional customs, or beliefs without realizing it. For example, some people believe that omens and superstitions can protect their lives instead of Jesus. Thus, they continue to indulge in such influences ignorantly. Christ does not require any cultural, religious, or additional object or symbol on your body as a token of faith for Him to bless you.

Negative influences, a pagan lifestyle, bad habits, and carnal behaviors such as greed and covetousness can cause defilement. The critical thing is to avoid negative people and inappropriate habits or behaviors (Galatians 5:19–21).

When "Sisera" (or any bad habit or friendship) visits your tent or territory, will you be able to realize that his seemingly cheerful presence and apparent haven in your tent will have costly repercussions in the future (Judges 4:14–24)? Otherwise, you must sever or avoid such alliances or agreements, just as Jael, the wife of Heber, did.

Just as the old covenant condemned and prohibited physical idol worship, we are called to be "separated" from the world today. This separation helps protect our hearts from the corruption of embracing a pagan lifestyle and its influences.

1 Peter 4:3-4 For we have spent enough of our past lifetime in doing the will of the Gentiles — when we walked in lewdness, lusts, drunkenness, revelries, drinking parties, and abominable idolatries. 4 In regard to these, they think it strange that you do not run with them in the same flood of dissipation, speaking evil of you.

Traditional customs and cultures, which are emphasized by many societies and family backgrounds but do not glorify God or the gospel, are also snares to divert our faith.

Mark 7:9 He said to them, "All too well you reject the commandment of God, that you may keep your tradition.

Whatever you do, or whatever you like or cherish, always ask yourself, "Is it in line with God's Word?" or, "Does it glorify God?" (Colossians 3:17).

We should also realize that carnality, or walking in worldly or fleshly desires, is a weapon that the devil uses to drift or pull people away from God (Luke 8:14).

Romans 8:7 Because the carnal mind is enmity against God; for it is not subject to the law of God, nor indeed can be. 8 So then, those who are in the flesh cannot please God.

Believers should safeguard themselves from hidden sins of the heart, which choke the Word inside. Christ highlighted that most carnal thoughts from our hearts may defile or corrupt us. If allowed to remain in our hearts, they may cause us to become unholy. Hatred, grudges, unforgiveness, bitterness, and falsehood are some of the many errors. We should not continue to keep such things in our hearts if we want our prayers to be fruitful and effective in our faith journey.

> **Proverbs 4:23** *Keep your heart with all diligence, For out of it spring the issues of life.*

Continuous exposure to such filth results in a defiled heart that needs cleansing by the Word.

> **Mark 7:18-23** *So He said to them, "Are you thus without understanding also? Do you not perceive that whatever enters a man from outside cannot defile him, 19 because it does not enter his heart but his stomach, and is eliminated, thus purifying all foods?" 20 And He said, "What comes out of a man, that defiles a man. 21 For from within, out of the heart of men, proceed evil thoughts, adulteries, fornications, murders, 22 thefts, covetousness, wickedness, deceit, lewdness, an evil eye, blasphemy, pride, foolishness. 23 All these evil things come from within and defile a man."*

Failure to address these issues severely limits the effectiveness of prayer in breaking spiritual strongholds such as family attacks, generational curses, financial and biological barrenness, health problems, and social enmities (Joshua 7:13). Impurity and a lack of knowledge are strongholds that the enemy uses to hold us back or hinder our prayers from being answered or yielding fruit.

We must guard our hearts diligently and purify ourselves with the Word (1 John 3:3) to win our spiritual battles through Christ. Also, remember that self-control begins in the mind. Believers safeguard themselves by rebuking and denouncing evil thoughts or a wayward mindset, which the devil uses to defile their hearts (2 Corinthians 10:4-5).

The good news is that consistent devotion will gradually dissolve these burdens through the Word of God as we remain in prayer.

A Thorn in the Flesh

This topic—A thorn in the flesh, 2 Corinthians 12:7-10—will be discussed in light of this book's overall theme to encourage spiritual virtue and make prayers more effective. This is so that we can overcome the enemy's spiritual resistance.

After considering the various weights of sin that may become a snare in our hearts, we should also realize that God will help us overcome them. This is only possible if we remain positive in our faith and pursue Christ more and more.

I will now look at the mindset, attitude, and approach that helped the apostle Paul combat discouragement from the enemy in an attempt to draw him away from serving in the gospel's ministry.

> *2 Corinthians 12:7-10 And lest I should be exalted above measure by the abundance of the revelations, a thorn in the flesh was given to me, a messenger of Satan to buffet me, lest I be exalted above measure. 8 Concerning this thing I pleaded with the Lord three times that it might depart from me. 9 And He said to me, "My grace is sufficient for you, for My strength is made perfect in weakness." Therefore, most gladly I will rather boast in my infirmities, that the power of Christ may rest upon me. 10 Therefore I take pleasure in infirmities, in reproaches, in needs,*

*in persecutions, in distresses, for Christ's sake. For when I am
weak, then I am strong.*

We can see in verse 7 that this thorn would restrict the apostle
from being exalted, as he still had to serve Christ in the gospel in
humility during that time. God sometimes allows us to be humbled
or teaches us to humble ourselves because He knows that when
the time is right, He will glorify His faithful children (1 Peter 5:6-7).
However, the apostle's experience, about which he speaks in verse
10, was one of weakness and pain that would eventually make him
strong in faith.

There are times when our weaknesses become thorns in our
lives. A thorn is a pain or drawback that drags down our
confidence, boldness, or courage and hinders us from moving
forward in the faith.

Here, the apostle used this painful experience or drawback as a
stepping stone for strengthening his faith and relying more on God
than his own abilities. Sometimes, God allows us to experience
tough times and struggles or become weaker (needy) so that we
learn to depend solely on Him. The virtue of enduring a test while
remaining faithful and steadfast in God builds character and
patience (Romans 5:3-6).

Your Thorn Should Not Lead You into Sin

In the same way, certain thorns creep into our lives before or
after we receive grace. These can draw us back or become snares
to our faith. It could be a disability, a lack of a life partner, an
unequal yoke in marriage, barrenness, sickness, and so on. Such
thorns come with negative or societal pressures that can lead you

to compromise your faith. Instead, learn to depend on God through your weaknesses.

But there are also self-imposed thorns. To take possession of the land of Canaan, the Israelites were commanded to completely drive out all the Canaanite inhabitants. The Lord spoke to Moses and said to him,

Numbers 33:51-52

"Speak to the children of Israel, and say to them: 'When you have crossed the Jordan into the land of Canaan, 52 then you shall drive out all the inhabitants of the land from before you, destroy all their engraved stones, destroy all their molded images, and demolish all their high places.

However, the Israelites did not entirely drive out the Gentiles from the Promised Land. The engraved images and idolatrous acts of the residue of the Gentiles who lived among them became a trap for the Israelites. And the Lord said to them:

Judges 2:3 "I will not drive them out before you, but they shall be thorns in your side, and their gods shall be a snare to you."

As time passed, the Israelites fell into the sin of idolatry and started to depend on other gods instead of the one true God. It is important to note that the thorn in Paul's situation differed from that faced by the Israelites; the latter endured a "self-imposed thorn," ultimately leading them to idolatry.

We would want to avoid a situation in which Christians are lured back to the "old man's habits" because of a thorn such as an unbelieving spouse, singleness (loneliness), or their employment circumstances. Many Christians overlook the pressures that accompany these setbacks and find themselves drawn into them, thereby succumbing to the enemy.

At some point, we have all experienced a thorn in our lives. This could stem from our life backgrounds, past errors, adverse influences, or wrong decisions that we have made. It could be negligence (self-imposed) or things beyond our control, as with the apostle Paul, such as disability, poor parenting, and difficult living conditions.

I view a "self-imposed thorn" as a condition of influence that directs or presses you toward carnal deeds or weights of sin that oppose God's Word. The Israelites yielded to the idolatrous acts of the surrounding nations and ended up in captivity. In their case, their thorn was the Gentiles living with them within their territory. They then 'yielded' to this thorn by committing idolatry, and the recurring act of worship became the weight of sin.

A self-imposed thorn will weigh you down and make you compromise your faith. If you are looking for a job and considering working for a company that makes you uncomfortable due to potential corrupt practices, you will have to rely entirely on God. You will have to depend on divine guidance to navigate the pressures of that job without compromising your values. If these pressures seem overwhelming and persistent, it may indicate that the job is a thorn in your life. You should pray and find ways to avoid succumbing to such shady deeds.

In the case of the Israelites (or believers), giving in to the thorn of embracing the Gentiles eventually led them into captivity by foreign nations. Similarly, believers who succumb to thorns will become spiritually dry or stagnant. Such thorns will hinder them from experiencing major life breakthroughs, which we earnestly desire from God every day.

Furthermore, we can see that a thorn is also an environment or condition of influence that pressures a person to yield to compromise.

The Compromise Becomes the Weight of Sin

Once the compromise becomes recurring or habitual, it becomes the weight of sin. It is now backsliding, just as the Israelites and the ten virgins did (Matthew 25:5). Yielding to the pressure of your thorn implies that some weight of sin emerges gradually. Such an obstacle or burden could be bitterness, unforgiveness, corrupt or shady business dealings, sexual immorality, adultery, envy, and more.

The apostle Paul used his thorn not as a barrier, but as a stepping stone to strengthen his faith. He was strengthened even though it was coming from physical suffering rather than a self-imposed error, as in the case of the Israelites mixing with Gentiles. Instead of allowing the thorn to weaken his faith, he turned to God for strength. In his weakness, he learned to depend on God.

We can also realize that, despite whatever weights, problems, challenges, barriers, or negative things that may have affected our lives, we get stronger through Christ and conquer them (2 Corinthians 12:9-10). The more difficult a situation is, the more we must depend solely on God. God wanted to make the Israelites confront and eliminate idolatry once and for all. However, they succumbed to this sin, and Christ had to come and restore them and us.

Christ's grace is sufficient to make us stronger when we are weak. Let no thorn hinder your progress as a believer when there is abundant grace through Christ to use that thorn as a stepping stone. Many people, including orphans, widows, and 'innocent' convicts, have reformed through grace, faith, and dependence on God. They have learned how to break away from bondage and help others escape similar challenges. It requires patience, determination, encouragement, and faith to eliminate any thorn that obstructs our path.

Are you suffering or experiencing any setbacks because of a thorn in your life? It could be a natural impairment, poor life decisions, an abusive spouse, unfair treatment from extended family, or the loss of a loved one.

- Don't give up on your faith and confidence. Arise and keep praying.
- Encourage yourself. Our faith is a journey. You shall break free one day, in Jesus' name.
- Depend on and call upon God for strength to continue in faith.

Thus, to show God's power and grace, believers must persist in removing thorns from their path and refuse to give in to such pressure. This is achievable through faith and dependency on God, just as the apostle Paul learned to continue relying on and looking up to Jesus, no matter how much pain he suffered.

Seven Tips on How to Tackle Thorns

The following key tips can help us deal with the thorns in our lives: A person once asked, "What makes a person great?"

This question depends on the context, just as Jesus' disciples asked Him, "Who is the greatest in the kingdom of God?"

A person who excels in wisdom, righteousness, and purity of heart (by grace) is far better than one who excels in overthrowing a city. If we humble ourselves and seek God, He will deposit the wisdom and knowledge to help us sail through our struggles through His Word.

Thus, the primary way for an individual to effectively overcome the influence of thorns in their lives is by seeking godly wisdom. This enlightens our understanding, allowing us to apply the Word to our daily lives and recognize areas where we may be going astray. Therefore:

1. You should cultivate a unique character that attracts God. As humans, we are not perfect, just like Jacob and Phinehas. However, these men exhibited a distinct character that set them apart. Jacob may not have possessed the same faith as Abraham, but he had the fervor of clinging to God, declaring that he would not let go until God blessed him (Genesis 32:24-31). Phinehas demonstrated the determination to confront those who had acted wickedly before God's wrath fell upon the children of Israel, and God blessed him (Numbers 25:7-13). Abraham had such immense faith that he traveled without knowing his destination, trusting God would lead him. Therefore, whatever admirable qualities you possess, please do not allow them

to go idle. For instance, if you regularly assist strangers, continue to do so. This is your contribution to this life, regardless of any other shortcomings you may have. Moreover, seven key actions can attract abundant blessings into your life. They are as follows:

i.   Putting God and His Word first.

ii. Maintaining a consistent prayer and devotional life is essential for gradual spiritual growth.

iii. Taking responsibility for God's work and doing it willingly (Colossians 3:23-24).

iv. As much as possible, seek peace, forgiveness, and fairness with everyone (Romans 12:18-19).

v.   Honoring parents, elders, and authorities (Titus 3:1-2).

vi. Assisting fellow believers by offering money, resources, or other means to enhance their lives and well-being, particularly within the Body of Christ. This is for their edification, spiritual growth, and gospel ministry.

Engaging in charity work, showing generosity, and cheerfully providing for those in need. This includes widows, orphans, the sick, the disabled, the oppressed, relatives, and those facing financial difficulties.

vii. Avoiding negative company, whether in friendships or other business or joint ventures.

2. Seek to align with God's Word (right standing with God) to prevent the enemy from gaining a foothold (Ephesians 4:27) to take advantage of your shortcomings, negligence, and lack of knowledge. Remember the misalignment of Samson (Judges 14:3)? He made poor choices in his marriage that ultimately caused him much pain. Be sensitive to your heart or inner self so that you can be comfortable with the decisions you make. Therefore, it's important to avoid being swayed to make unwise decisions in life.

3. Seek godly advice and counsel from fellow members of the Body of Christ who are faithful and more seasoned in the Word and faith than you (Proverbs 20:18; 24:6).

4. Be aware and safeguard yourself from any weight of sin through random self-introspection.

   __Hebrews 12:1__ Therefore we also, since we are surrounded by so great a cloud of witnesses, let us lay aside every weight, and the sin which so easily ensnares us, and let us run with endurance the race that is set before us, 2 looking unto Jesus, ...

You do not want your heart to be carried away by the pollution of this fast-moving world, be it carnal human nature, social media, or other "elements" of the world.

We should conduct regular self-assessments to maintain a healthy relationship with God. Receiving God's grace to live by faith in Christ does not eliminate temptation. Christ has set us free, but the enemy will always try to use our past errors or weaknesses to draw our faith backward. Yes, old things have passed away, but we must always open our eyes and be sensitive to our inner man. This is to identify and take steps to safeguard our lives from falling into the same old traps.

Some of the common weights that the enemy uses to hinder spiritual growth in believers are:

i.   Lust—sexual impurity, desire for the things and pleasures of the world, reveling, jovial rioting, etc.

ii. Greed—materialism and covetousness; and excess—by things like addiction, drugs, alcoholism, etc.

iii. Corruption, deceit, falsehood, and flattery.

iv. Vain traditions and beliefs, cultural superstition, sorcery, witchcraft, and idolatry.

v.   Pride and vain ambitions.

vi. Grudges, malice, bitterness, hatred, envy, jealousy, strife, disputes, wrath, emulation, and slander.

vii. Fear, a lack of positivity or faith and trust in God, and impatience.

viii. Prayerlessness, slothfulness, filthiness, and disorderliness.

ix. Faith without works of love (the priest and the good Samaritan, Luke 10:25-37). Beliefs and doctrines that deviate from the gospel and do not demonstrate sincerity, love, and concern for those in need.

x.   Unequal yoke in marriages. Unjustified joint ventures.

The list of common sins can help believers evaluate their faith and identify weaknesses. One can become more alert and diligent in prayer to walk circumspectly and lay aside any weight of sin that may creep into his life. It is about being sincere and truthful to oneself and God. He allows us to **focus on** what needs rectification through repentance, prayer, and diligence.

5. Avoid blaming others for your situation, even if they have done something wrong. Sometimes the enemy uses or influences other people to fight you. Believers should know they are fighting a spiritual battle rather than confronting others. Because of that, stay calm, especially in your heart. David did not hold grudges against Saul, although Saul repeatedly attempted to take his life (1 Samuel 24:4-6). Keep your thoughts positive and avoid self-destructive thoughts. God still loves you, and all things work together for good (Romans 8:28).
6. Commit your situation to God. Exalt and pray to God, knowing He is in control, casting all your care upon Him, for He cares for you (1 Peter 5:7).
7. Be courageous as you move forward in steps of discretion and faith (1 Samuel 30:6-10, 18).

Summary (key points)

Isaiah 60:1-3 Arise, shine; For your light has come! And the glory of the LORD is risen upon you. 2 For behold, the darkness shall cover the earth, And deep darkness the people; But the LORD will arise over you, And His glory will be seen upon you. 3 The Gentiles shall come to your light, And kings to the brightness of your rising.

▪ By identifying the thorns (and the weight of sin) that the devil has deposited in his life, a believer can free himself from the devil's suppression. He has to renounce such weights and rise up (or breakaway) through boldness and faith to run the race of true faith (Hebrews 12:1).

- As he approaches the throne of grace through consistent and regular prayer, he must diligently ensure that he grows spiritually through the Word. He can achieve this by applying its teachings in his life (2 John 6). In other words, his good deeds should reflect a sound faith and a fruitful spirit. The qualities of genuine faith—such as trust in God, fear of God, steadfastness, joy, gratitude, perseverance, love, faith, patience, and self-control—will begin to manifest and flourish. As a result, he is able to make wise decisions, succeed, and regain many of the blessings and benefits that the adversary had taken away from him.

- Then, realizing God's purpose in his life, he steps into it. Thus, being led by Christ and allowing God to make the shining light in him become a positive influence in transforming people's lives.

CHAPTER 2

STEPS TO ESTABLISH A FIRM

FOUNDATION OF FAITH

Many people struggle to maintain a regular prayer life. This is because the enemy is at work trying to hinder prayer and meditation from effectively working to yield spiritual growth and the fruit of the Spirit, like love, faith, and patience, through unwavering faith in Christ. Devotion is a phenomenal process that fosters growth in Christians, allowing them to find strength in life's struggles while also recognizing the goodness of God. As a result, they become motivated to continue thriving and to seek more of God's presence and goodness in their lives.

In this chapter, I will share essential tips for embracing unwavering faith and highlight key areas to safeguard as a believer. The goal is to maintain a devotional life that promotes spiritual growth and draws us closer to God. Hence it is essential to avoid allowing our faith to become stagnant or reduced to a mere tradition that lacks the desired fruit of righteous deeds. By doing so, we are becoming better and drawing closer to God spiritually.

Faith can become a stagnant religion because of two main reasons:

a) **Lack of spiritual growth**: Make regular self-assessments to see whether you are growing spiritually.

b) **Inability to engage in spiritual warfare or resist temptations against the enemy**: Be instant in and out of season. This is through alertness as you continue in prayer and obedience to the Word without yielding to temptation or error (1 Peter 2:11).

The following are key points that will help a believer's prayer and devotional life become more effective and lead to sanctification and spiritual growth:

1) <u>The Fear of God</u>

The fear of God is the unwavering and steadfast adherence to your faith values in accordance with God's Word through a mindset of reverent submission to God's will while resisting and avoiding evil. This person will love God because the fear of God makes a person abide in and pursue God's Word as their first and principal priority.

To win the spiritual battle, believers should grow in grace and the Word of God while remaining steadfast and unmovable in their faith (Ephesians 6:10-18).

> *<u>1 Corinthians 15:58</u> Therefore, my beloved brethren, be steadfast, immovable, always abounding in the work of the Lord,*

knowing that your labor is not in vain in the Lord.

We must adopt the spirit and mindset of not giving the enemy any opportunity or foothold.

__Ephesians 4:27__ ..., nor give place to the devil.

Instead, develop a culture of abstaining from and eschewing evil.

__1 Thessalonians 5:22__ Abstain from every form of evil.

We can only attain this culture through the fear of God. This is accomplished by developing an upright conscience that seeks to please God.

__Hebrews 13:18__ Pray for us; for we are confident that we have a good conscience, in all things desiring to live honourably.

The more we become steadfast in exercising our senses to shun evil and act upon God's Word, the more God will uplift and strengthen us spiritually (Mark 4:24-25, 9:49).

__1 Peter 5:8-9__ Be sober, be vigilant; because your adversary the devil walks about like a roaring lion, seeking whom he may devour. 9 Resist him, steadfast in the faith, knowing that the same sufferings are experienced by your brotherhood in the world.

We see that a person who fears God will always resist falling into sin. The Bible has examples of people who strengthened their relationship with God because of their steadfastness and refusal to yield to sin.

__Job 27:6__ My righteousness I hold fast, and will not let it go; My heart shall not reproach me as long as I live.

A person like Job became closer to God because of his hatred of sin (Job 1:5) and his zeal for being righteous before God. For this reason, the devil was not fighting Job's physical riches (Job 2:9-10) but was fighting the fruit of righteousness in Job (Job 23:11-12). The root of this fruit is "holding fast," as we see in Job's own words in the above verse.

Daniel chose to eat basic food instead of the king's special food because he did not want to defile himself (Daniel 1:8). Together with his friends, they resisted the pressure to worship idols, even to the point of death, because of their fear of God and steadfastness (Daniel 3:14-26).

Joseph's lifestyle and character revealed the fear of God, as he testified:

> **Genesis 39:9** *There is no one greater in this house than I, nor has he kept back anything from me but you, because you are his wife. How then can I do this great wickedness, and sin against God?"*

This resulted in God being with him and granting him success in all his endeavors (Genesis 39:1-6, 21). He suffered through hardships, temptations, and persecutions, yet despite all these, he did not yield to sin because of the fear of God (Genesis 39:8-9). We can also see that Joseph was spiritually sensitive to God's will because of his upright conscience and love. After all the harsh treatment from his brothers, he responded to them in love by telling them that God intended their evil for good.

> **Genesis 50:19-20** *Joseph said to them, "Do not be afraid, for am I in the place of God? 20 But as for you, you meant evil against me; but God meant it for good, in order to bring it about as it is this day, to save many people alive.*

Through God's grace, he focused on the welfare of his family and brothers and did not hold on to their evil deeds in his heart. To maintain that steadfast mindset of shunning evil, we should ask God to help us deal with past 'evil' experiences or grudges that could drag us backward.

Because Joseph feared God, he steadfastly resisted the temptation of Potiphar's wife. Because he crossed this hurdle, God elevated him from being a prisoner to becoming a minister of Pharaoh in Egypt.

Many people become complacent, hesitant, or even comfortable with immorality. However, if you do not boldly confront and reject bad habits from deep within your heart, you will eventually succumb to them, whether you want to or not. It's crucial to take a decisive stand and commit to your values.

According to Ephesians 5:15-16, we live in perilous times and should walk circumspectly. To attain the "strong food" of the Word of God or understand the deeper teachings of the Bible, believers must grow in faith and exercise their conscience and sense of discernment (Hebrews 5:12-14) to avoid evil. This will prevent them from falling easily during trials, tests, or temptations.

Exhibiting God's fear entails having a healthy respect for God's Word. It also includes perceiving and rejecting wickedness, avoiding evil, and coming to sincere repentance if you commit a transgression. We need to abide in God's love by pursuing His will and obeying His Word.

2) <u>Trust in God</u>

<u>*Psalms 37:3-5*</u>

3 Trust in the Lord, and do good;

Dwell in the land, and feed on His faithfulness.

4 Delight yourself also in the Lord,

And He shall give you the desires of your heart.

5 Commit your way to the Lord,

Trust also in Him,

And He shall bring it to pass.

<u>*Proverbs 3:5-6*</u>

5 Trust in the Lord with all your heart,

And lean not on your own understanding;

6 In all your ways acknowledge Him,

And He shall direct your paths.

One of the most critical pillars of our comfort and refuge is trust in and dependency on God, knowing He will never forsake us. A Christian should always depend on and lean on God, no matter how big or small the task or conflict. This is because we know Christ is always with us and interceding for us (John 14:18; Hebrews 13:5; 1 Peter 5:7). God is our refuge, and we must always trust Him (Psalm 91:1-16).

<u>*Psalms 91:2-6*</u>

2 I will say of the LORD, "He is my refuge and my fortress;

My God, in Him I will trust.

3 Surely He shall deliver you from the snare of the fowler

And from the perilous pestilence.

4 He shall cover you with His feathers,

And under His wings you shall take refuge;

His truth shall be your shield and buckler.

5 You shall not be afraid of the terror by night,

Nor of the arrow that flies by day,

6 Nor of the pestilence that walks in darkness,

Nor of the destruction that lays waste at noonday.

Protection

We are overcomers by faith and the blood of the Lamb, for our salvation, deliverance, healing, breakthroughs, and so on. However, if we want to have that covering, protection, and refuge of God in our walk in the faith, we need to develop and have that trust in God.

> *Proverbs 29:25 The fear of man brings a snare, But whosoever trusts in the LORD shall be safe.*

When the waves of spiritual attacks begin to roar and your beloved ones encounter sickness and the fear of death, or your employment is uncertain, or your business is plunging, look up to God with a bold heart and a psalm of praise, through trust in Him.

<u>Psalms 46</u>

1 God is our refuge and strength, A very present help in trouble.

2 Therefore we will not fear, Even though the earth be removed, And though the mountains be carried into the midst of the sea;

3 Though its waters roar and be troubled, Though the mountains shake with its swelling. Selah

Overcoming in Battle

The Bible has many examples of faithful people who conquered and won battles because they relied on God.

> <u>2 Chronicles 14:11-12</u> *And Asa cried out to the Lord his God, and said, "Lord, it is nothing for You to help, whether with many or with those who have no power; help us, O Lord our God, for we rest on You, and in Your name, we go against this multitude. O Lord, You are our God; do not let man prevail against You!" 12 So the Lord struck the Ethiopians before Asa and Judah, and the Ethiopians fled.*

However, when things get tough or the path to success seems unlikely, many believers try to complement God's grace with their own efforts. They do this by collaborating with external means or sources contrary to God's Word. Our faith should triumph over tempestuous winds or troubles in daily life. We can see from the passage that King Asa won his battles because he called upon and relied on God. However, as the years progressed, he lost sight of this concept of faith and trust in the Lord. He made a league with the king of Syria, which cost him years of peace thereafter.

2 Chronicles 16:7-9 And at that time Hanani the seer came to Asa king of Judah, and said to him: "Because you have relied on the king of Syria, and have not relied on the Lord your God, therefore the army of the king of Syria has escaped from your hand. 8 Were the Ethiopians and the Lubim not a huge army with very many chariots and horsemen? Yet, because you relied on the Lord, He delivered them into your hand. 9 For the eyes of the Lord run to and fro throughout the whole earth, to show Himself strong on behalf of those whose heart is loyal to Him. In this you have done foolishly; therefore, from now on you shall have wars."

"No one who looks back is fit for God's kingdom," says Christ (Luke 9:62).

Have you ever felt like reverting to your past ways of life when things were going well? Do you ever admire non-believers who are prosperous in their businesses or ventures? Do you sometimes copy or emulate their ways or devices? When you do this, you are diverting your focus from God and losing your full trust in Him. Your major success is being fully alive in the Light within you (Colossians 1:27). God may restrict our path as we run the race. This is because He wants us to witness a miracle from Him when we overcome such obstacles through His hand so that His name is glorified.

God deliberately led the Israelites into the wilderness on their journey from Egypt to Canaan, where food and water were scarce. He wanted them to learn to look up to Him, depend on Him, and expect His stretched-out arm to succor them in times of need, which He did (Psalms 78:1-72). However, their hearts still looked back to Egypt's provisions instead of Him. Because of this, God was unhappy (1 Corinthians 10:5; Hebrews 3:7-12).

God is faithful and never abandons us. Therefore, believers should avoid reverting to their old ways or being inspired by the seemingly prosperous paths of unbelievers. If we focus on God and strive to fulfill His purposes, He will fight our battles for us.

A believer should seek God's guidance and blessings before pursuing a career, business, or even family or matrimonial matters, just as Jacob did.

> *Genesis 32:26 And He said, "Let Me go, for the day breaks." But he said, "I will not let You go unless You bless me!",*

We must always seek peace of mind when we look forward to the promises that await us, knowing that God is in control as a loving and sovereign Father who cares for us.

> *Colossians 3:15 And let the peace of God rule in your hearts, to which also were are called in one body; and be thankful,*

To know that, in whatever situations or challenges, "GOD IS IN CHARGE" and "GOD IS AT WORK," to ensure His purpose is fulfilled through us. This is only possible if we yield to Him and trust in Him.

Some difficulties or failures could strengthen or keep us from going astray by preventing our souls from sinning when we do not see or perceive the hidden traps in those "enticing opportunities." Eventually, we will glorify God (Romans 8:28).

Instead of getting frustrated when eagerly anticipated breakthroughs seem to vanish into thin air as if God is unaware of them, let believers delight in God. This is because God's timing is always the right time for everything they ask of Him. They must look up to Him, stand firm, and obey His statutes. Otherwise, they risk taking alternative options that become costly for them. This was the case with King Saul, who failed to wait patiently for Samuel to arrive and offer peace and burnt offerings. Instead, he performed the offering himself, which God had forbidden.

> *1 Samuel 13:8-14 Then he waited seven days, according to the time set by Samuel. But Samuel did not come to Gilgal; and the people were scattered from him. 9 So Saul said, "Bring a burnt offering and peace offerings here to me." And he offered the burnt offering. 10 Now it happened, as soon as he had finished presenting the burnt offering, that Samuel came; and Saul went out to meet him, that he might greet him.*

> *13 And Samuel said to Saul, "You have done foolishly. You have not kept the commandment of the Lord your God, which He commanded you. For now the Lord would have established your kingdom over Israel forever. 14 But now your kingdom shall not continue.*

Yes, the grace to be reconciled back to God after falling short is in abundance through Christ Jesus (Luke 15:21-24; 1 John 1:9). However, missing a breakthrough because of negligence or disobedience can be hard to recover from (Judges 16:20-30), even after reconciling back to the true faith. We see that impatience, doubt, and unbelief are undesirable characteristics in God's eyes (Numbers 14:6-12; Matthew 14:29-32). A lack of trust in God can cause you to miss out on spiritual and livelihood breakthroughs.

Waiting on God Requires Discipline

As previously mentioned, there are times when our desired breakthroughs take a long time to materialize. During these times, thoughts about why life is becoming monotonous and stagnant enter our minds. If such is the case, we should ask ourselves whether we are in line with God's plan. We should also ask whether we ever committed our desires to God. While there is always abundant grace, whenever you strive for success in any aspect of life, such as family, finances, business, or work, it is important to ask yourself the following questions:

- Will your future perspective be a blessing to others, and does it glorify God?
- Will you learn to depend on God to show discipline and faithfulness without quickly reverting to unruly shortcuts when things don't go your way?
- Do you truly have a heart for what you are pursuing, so that you will continue to put in more effort regardless of negative results, or is it just out of convenience?
- What is God, or the Word of God, saying to you in that area of pursuit?

Let God mold you so that when you achieve a breakthrough, you can handle it with humility and be a blessing to others (James 4:3-4). One can be highly confident and enthusiastic about pursuing a venture, mission, or any other desire.

There is also a need to pray or seek God's guidance and the spirit of wisdom to discern God's timing or recognize the right season. In this way, you avoid premature actions or endeavors that typically fail and ultimately demotivate you. This is just as Moses killed the Egyptian in an attempt to deliver and free the children of Israel from slavery (Acts 7:24-29). He failed at the time and ran away from Pharaoh to reside in the land of the Midianites. When the time was right, God sent Moses back to Egypt to deliver the Israelites from captivity by God's hand.

It is common for some people to become too impatient with success without allowing themselves enough time for self-growth. Rushing for success without developing character, discipline, faith, and reliance on God can be detrimental. Missing the proper timing to undertake a venture, even if it's your true destiny according to God's plan, might make you fail prematurely. This is if you lack the spiritual sensitivity to discern God's timing. It is not only about patience, but also about judgment, discernment, and circumspection.

While we always say God's timing is right, you can also prolong God's timing if you do not allow Him to mold you with the character and discipline that will enable you to grab, receive, and move with the desired breakthrough or blessing. Some people possess exceptional talent and skills but lack the ability to communicate, collaborate, or work cooperatively with their fellows. This can be costly, as collaboration and effective communication are usually the key drivers in any organization.

It is important to let God mold or help us manage those minor obstacles we often ignore. If not addressed, these can be consequential, delaying our breakthroughs.

Thus, there is a need for the *spirit of excellence* that Daniel had (Daniel 6:1-5). This is:

- Possession of a good character or personality and being able to handle life's challenges, tasks, or work within a society (usually in a social environment) through discipline, temperance, and modesty,

— with skill and thoroughness in everything that you do, while

— taking due responsibility and diligence,

— in a way that pleases God, so that His name is glorified in you.

The Bible says Daniel was distinguished above all the selected governors in King Darius' kingdom. He was faithful, with no error or fault being found in him. If we also move in the same spirit in whatever we do, we will also obtain God's favor, and He will push us through to abound and excel.

If we approach life in this way, we will succeed in our endeavors. Take a moment to be still, discern, or hear God speaking to you to identify areas of improvement in your circumstances and activities. Continue to ask God for guidance on how to succeed in your endeavors.

Fundamental Steps to Build or Root Your Trust in God

- Commit your plans to God and ask for His guidance (Psalms 37:5-7).
- Do not act hastily to carry out or pursue your goals; instead, exercise extra caution until you are sure and comfortable with your decisions and objectives, and then act wisely.
- Do not be quick to reveal your plans or intentions to others except to those you trust, especially in the faith. This is what King Hezekiah did to expose the treasures in the House of God to the Babylonians (2 Kings 20:12-18).

- Believe that you are safe in God's hands and that He will never forsake you (Hebrews 13:5).
- See beyond the limits. To trust God, one must not feel bound or constrained by their current circumstances. Be positive and believe God will change your situation for your good and His glory. Trust the Word of God more than what you see with your eyes because God can change the circumstances you see right now. In this regard, speak positive words and have positive thoughts.

  > ***Numbers 14:6-9*** *But Joshua the son of Nun and Caleb the son of Jephunneh, who were among those who had spied out the land, tore their clothes; 7 and they spoke to all the congregation of the children of Israel, saying: "The land we passed through to spy out is an exceedingly good land. 8 If the LORD delights in us, then He will bring us into this land and give it to us, 'a land which flows with milk and honey.' 9 Only do not rebel against the LORD, nor fear the people of the land, for they are our bread; their protection has departed from them, and the LORD is with us. Do not fear them."*

  Though the children of Israel were discouraged by their perception of the gigantic men of Anak, Joshua and Caleb saw things differently. These two men had faith and trusted in God. Hence, do not let your mind limit your calling or restrict you from reaching your destiny.

- By asking yourself if you are genuinely prepared in terms of capacity or maturity, you can be at peace with your motives and actions. You may proceed if you feel comfortable and confident (Romans 14:22).

- Be positive and ready to digest the outcome of your efforts, whether positive or negative. This will help you learn from your experience and understand what God wants you to know. Continue pushing and trying unless you realize a better plan from God.

Do not lose hope; remain courageous and look to Jesus, knowing God will help you. He is always with us to see us push through because, eventually, He will stretch forth His hand to fulfill His promises in our lives.

3) Praising and Being Thankful to God

The Lord Jesus Christ is the source of joy for all believers (Philippians 4:4).

> *1 Thessalonians 5:18 In everything give thanks; for this is the will of God in Christ Jesus for you.*

Why? Because salvation can never be compared to anything in this life. We need to be illuminated and see the reconciliation Christ has accomplished for us, not only on the Cross but by sanctifying us daily so that we can eventually enjoy His eternal glory (Ephesians 1:1-23).

We do not want to wait for our breakthroughs to manifest before thanking and praising God. We honor Him for who He is, His sovereignty, and His love. He has redeemed us to become sons through Christ. He desires that we grow spiritually into His likeness.

Thus, our praises extend before us, alongside our spiritual battles and fights, and thereafter. Remember that God once led the children of Israel to overthrow Jericho by encompassing it with praise continuously for seven days (Joshua 6:1-21). Remember that a sincere heart of praise can move God to release your breakthrough (Acts 16:25-31; 1 Samuel 16:23).

The children of Israel were ungrateful to God during their journey from Egypt to the Promised Land. This was one of their biggest errors, along with forgetting God's covenant and looking back to Egypt. Their constant complaints and confrontations with Moses led to their overthrow in the wilderness by God, as He was not pleased with them (1 Corinthians 10:1-11). As a result, many did not receive the promise (Hebrews 3:19).

Whatever difficulties we face, we should always live in praise and thanksgiving to God.

> *Hebrews 13:15 Therefore by Him let us continually offer the sacrifice of praise to God, that is, the fruit of our lips, giving thanks to His name.*
>
> *1 Thessalonians 5:18 In everything give thanks; for this is the will of God in Christ Jesus for you.*
>
> *Ephesians 5:19-20 speaking to one another in psalms and hymns and spiritual songs, singing and making melody in your heart to the Lord, 20 giving thanks always for all things to God the Father in the name of our Lord Jesus Christ.*
>
> (1 Peter 2:9-10).

Being thankful to God will always help us in the following ways:

- It is a form of praise and worship (Psalm 103:1).
- It attracts more blessings (Psalm 103:2).
- It draws us closer to Him (Psalm 103:3).

- It helps us endure and find deliverance during difficult times (Psalm 103:4).
- It gives us courage and drives us forward in all seasons (Psalm 103:5).

A heart that testifies to God's goodness moves God's heart. This is especially true when we see and appreciate His stretched arm helping us in times of need. Many seem more focused on the "specific" challenges they face daily. At the same time, we do not acknowledge, realize, or otherwise perceive previous breakthroughs over hurdles and challenges in other previous periods or timeframes that God has pulled us through. Acknowledge and thank God for helping you overcome challenges, despite having other areas where you may still need help.

God's Benefits Are Abundant

Psalm 103 is a motivational passage when it comes to praising God.

Psalm 103:1-5

1 Bless the LORD, O my soul;

And all that is within me, bless His holy name!

2 Bless the LORD, O my soul,

And forget not all His benefits:

3 Who forgives all your iniquities,

Who heals all your diseases,

4 Who redeems your life from destruction,

Who crowns you with lovingkindness and tender mercies,

5 Who satisfies your mouth with good things,

So that your youth is renewed like the eagle's.

We may now look at the verses:

❖ Psalms 103:1 - Exalting His Name

We bless, exalt, and magnify the LORD from within our hearts. We also pour out our hearts to the LORD in praise.

❖ Psalms 103:2-5 - His Lovingkindness and Benefits

God's benefits are more than abundant, especially when we acknowledge and realize His love for us. We also realize the undeserved grace we have received and how He has redeemed and reconciled us to Himself through the Cross and the blood of His Son, Jesus. Such benefits are also mentioned in verses 3-5, including the forgiveness of sins, healing, being redeemed from destruction, His tender mercies and lovingkindness, provisions, and prolonged life. When you praise, think about such benefits.

❖ Psalms 103: 8-10 - Mercy and Forgiveness

8 The LORD is merciful and gracious,

Slow to anger, and abounding in mercy.

9 He will not always strive with us,

Nor will He keep His anger forever.

10 He has not dealt with us according to our sins,

Nor punished us according to our iniquities.

God will not hold on to or keep in mind our transgressions. For this reason, we will confidently approach the throne of grace with thanksgiving and praise, and keep running the race of faith, despite our past mistakes.

17 But the mercy of the LORD is from everlasting to everlasting

On those who fear Him,

And His righteousness to children's children,

18 To such as keep His covenant, and to those who remember His commandments to do them.

But we should also remember that we must fear God by keeping His commandments (verse 18).

By expressing our sincere thanks to God for His mercy, love, and goodness, we acknowledge all that He has done for us. This includes His provision of health, elevation, protection, and other benefits. We also thank God for the gift of life and salvation through Christ.

❖ <u>Sacrificial Praise</u>

In tough times when life seems hopeless, keep looking to God as your source of strength and hope. He has promised never to forsake us (Hebrews 13:5). When you feel you are waiting too long for an answer to your prayers, remember God's love and His past blessings in your life.

The prophet Habakkuk says:

<u>***Habakkuk 3:17-18***</u>

17 Though the fig tree may not blossom,

Nor fruit be on the vines;

Though the labor of the olive may fail,

And the fields yield no food;

Though the flock may be cut off from the fold,

And there be no herd in the stalls —

18 Yet I will rejoice in the Lord,

I will joy in the God of my salvation.

In the above scripture, the prophet encourages us to praise the Lord God, who is our salvation and worthy of praise, regardless of any situation we face. Therefore, we should focus on Him, His love, and His goodness rather than the challenges themselves. Let us keep a positive attitude, especially an appreciation of the good things that God has done for us. As much as we encourage each other to cultivate a culture of aiming higher or striving for more in everything we do, we should ensure that our hearts are filled with godly contentment. This implies being always thankful and acknowledging God with the 'Ebenezer' mindset that "thus far, God has helped" (1 Samuel 7:12).

CHAPTER 3

UNLOCKING THE POWER:
Prayer and Spiritual Growth the Key to Victory in Spiritual Warfare

This chapter will discuss how spiritual virtue and prayer can help overcome spiritual conflicts through faith. Spiritual growth helps us attain a personality of virtue that overcomes the devil's resistance to salvation.

Spiritual growth for believers often faces resistance, as the devil seeks to hinder them from reaching a higher level of glory. He attempts to weaken and divert their focus, much like he did with the 'foolish virgins' in Matthew 25:8. Additionally, the parable of the unprofitable servant illustrates how an unfaithful servant failed to endure and fulfill his assigned mission due to a lack of faith and the challenges he encountered along the way (Matthew 25:24-30).

Therefore, individual spiritual growth is essential for overcoming the spiritual battles that arise in a believer's faith journey.

Spiritual Warfare: The Biggest Faith Hurdle

Spiritual warfare is mainly about the devil's attempts to weaken a believer's faith (1 Peter 5:8-9). It is critical to grow spiritually to overcome such resistance and opposition. Therefore, spiritual warfare is about gaining spiritual virtue or genuine faith in Christ through fruit-bearing while handling and counteracting the enemy's resistance. It entails growing in Christ through the knowledge of God's Word and prayer and knowing how to respond and counteract the enemy's attacks, opposition, or challenges in a way that makes you continue fulfilling what God expects of you according to His Word (Ephesians 5:14-17).

The most basic form of spiritual attack is the enemy's influence to make a person accept what is wrong as right and right as wrong. So the first spiritual attack was the devil's influence on Eve. This is to make her oppose the instruction that God gave Adam, telling him not to eat the forbidden fruit in the Garden of Eden (Genesis 3:4-5). He aims to cause misalignment with God's Word.

The enemy's greatest battleground lies within the mind, where thoughts and beliefs can be influenced. His negative influences incite wayward thoughts, negativity, a mentality that contradicts God's Word, and a lack of prayer. As a result, the devil will constantly oppose and battle believers, mainly through the methods listed below:

1. Persecuting the Church

The enemy tries to inflict pain and fear so that we gradually lose courage, strength, focus, hope, and faith in God. He also attempts to scatter the believers from moving in oneness in the faith of the gospel (1 Peter 5:8-9). He accuses believers in order to demotivate them from pressing on in prayer and faith (Revelation 12:10).

2. Carnality (worldly lusts and a corrupt mindset)

Carnal behavior, a self-centered mentality, and fleshly desires replace the fulfillment of God's Word and will in a person's life, rendering it either void or unimportant. Such carnality comes in different forms, such as pride, slander, hatred, adultery, and greed (Mark 4:18-19).

3. Deceiving the World

The idea behind deception by the enemy is mainly to keep people away from the illumination of the light of the gospel or to lead people astray from the truth of the Word of God.

> *__2 Corinthians 4:3-4__ But even if our gospel is veiled, it is veiled to those who are perishing, 4 whose minds the god of this age has blinded, who do not believe, lest the light of the gospel of the glory of Christ, who is the image of God, should shine on them.*

The enemy tries to shun a believer's realization of who he is in Christ. Beware of false concepts, perceptions, notions, or teachings that replace or otherwise oppose God's Word. Many people follow individuals or even idols instead of the Lord Christ Himself. As a result, the majority have gone astray by accepting man's deeds and words rather than the Word of God. In the last days, the enemy will come with a "strong wind" of delusion. He tries to lure people away from the true faith by using subtle methods, fake miracles, and persuasive speeches of false teachers, leading the congregants astray from the Word of God (Acts 20:29-30).

The devil aims to divert attention from prayer to lead believers and the general populace astray from seeking God's presence. To accomplish this aim, he stirs up unbelief, causes error in the Word of God, and then replaces it with false teachings, customary beliefs, and philosophy.

Consequently, the journey of faith that ensures sanctification and spiritual growth calls for us to resist all these obstacles.

Gaining Confidence in Christ in the Face of Spiritual Opposition

It is important to realize that the devil frequently and objectively wears out believers spiritually. His aim is that they lose inspiration, become frustrated, and stop engaging in spiritual activities such as regular prayer, meditation, serving the Lord, and attending to people's needs. He wants to:

- Drain your zeal for God's work, either by keeping you preoccupied with worldly pursuits such as work, family issues, bad company, carnal hobbies, and idleness,
- Or else wear you down mentally through stress, peer pressure, and discouragement. This is so that you look down on yourself when things do not seem to go your way, either spiritually or because of personal life challenges. He aims to influence your mind so that you take actions contrary to the Word of God.
- Hinder your growth, particularly by preventing you from perceiving and discerning the various subtle temptations

coming your way. These temptations can easily be identified through the knowledge of God's Word and can also choke your prayer and devotional life.

- Persecute you to prevent you from impacting and uplifting others through the gospel message. He might even try to cause sickness in your family, as it was with Job, or stir up a wind of confusion at your workplace so that you live in fear.
- And, above all, hinder the realization of Christ as the answer, the refuge, and the redeemer of our lives.

In other words, the enemy buys time so that you do not get time to become spiritually sound and mature in character, personality, experience, and knowledge. This is to get you used to that 'casual' lifestyle. Because of this, such a believer will struggle to overcome trials and temptation.

Christ died on the cross for our reconciliation. This is so that we can live, not for ourselves, through the sinful influence and nature of this world, but according to His Word and in His presence (2 Corinthians 5:15). We have two opposing forces based on the following principles:

God's view: "Cross that hurdle of spiritual resistance as you minister in obedience to Christ, and I will bless you (2 Corinthians 4:17-18; Job 42:10)."

The devil's view: "Refuse God's ways and virtues and follow your own desires, traditions, or philosophy, and that is your freedom."

The reality of the second view is that most people continue to follow and trust persuasive worldly teachings, be they customs, traditions, or philosophy, rather than God's Word (Colossians 2:20-23; Mark 7:9), despite being oppressed.

As we pursue God's view, blessings manifest and come as we continue in faith. Hence, believers need to be consistent, prayerful, and continuously grow to overcome hurdles and obstacles that come along the way (2 Corinthians 4:15-17).

Thus, spiritual warfare starts in the mind through bad influence and carnal reasoning to divert a person from abiding by God's Word. When the enemy limits prayer and devotion, believers can become stagnant and struggle with insight, wisdom, and steadfastness.

We see that when a believer engages in prayer, they must not only focus on the outcome or results. They must also pray for grace to understand the root cause of the spiritual warfare they are encountering. For example, as Daniel, Ezra, and Nehemiah prayed for Israel's deliverance from the Babylonians, they also addressed and confessed Israel's sin of embracing foreign gods.

a) <u>God wants to bless us through serving Him in holiness</u>

God wants us to serve in ministry as vessels of honor according to our calling. This is so that we may glorify His name and attain perfection through obedience to His will. This will also open up doors for blessings in our lives. Whenever we glorify God's name, He blesses us, exalts us in due season, graces us for a supernatural breakthrough, and makes us spiritually fruitful. Your level of faith determines the dimension and level of the blessing or breakthrough (Ephesians 6:16).

Our faith grows when we confidently proclaim the name of Jesus in any situation that we encounter while having our hearts focused on living by God's Word. At such a stage, we can safely say, "We are overcomers, and no weapon formed against us can prosper (Isaiah-54:17)."

The Bible says that God will not allow the enemy to tempt us beyond our means (1 Corinthians 10:13). If we are growing spiritually or have matured spiritually, the level of challenges or temptations we will face will also be higher than before. For this reason, one of the most crucial qualities required for spiritual growth is the ability to resist, fight, and endure temptations. These wear us down or divert us from true faith.

The most basic way to serve God is through prayer and devotion to allow transformation within you as you abide in His love. Devotion fuels the believer's transformation continuously. It helps them grow spiritually (especially in wisdom and knowledge) to be ready for upcoming battles and remain steadfast in their faith.

Sanctification through devotion will aid spiritual growth in the following ways:

- ✓ Improving personality and character (good works or fruit-bearing through the Spirit).
- ✓ Gaining maturity and experience to remain steadfast in trials and temptations.
- ✓ Growing in knowledge, wisdom, and spiritual understanding of the Word to handle situations wisely and serve God according to His will.
- ✓ Learning to follow the guidance of the Word and the Spirit.

✓ It makes you look up to Christ rather than revert to the old life.

b) <u>Our victory is in looking to Jesus</u>

Many believe that in order to conquer spiritual battles, you must comprehend complex mysteries and how dark spiritual forces work. Yes, this is good and encouraged by God. However, to win spiritual warfare, rely on God's Word and study it; pray constantly; obey His Word; have faith; and allow Christ's guidance in your life (Ephesians 6:10-20).

Spiritual growth helps a Christian remain standing in the face of adversity. The "inner man" controls and resists the carnal nature as they progress through Christ. The key is to position yourself so that you continue hearing and obeying the voice or Word of God.

> <u>*John 10:27-28*</u> *My sheep hear My voice, and I know them, and they follow Me. 28 And I give them eternal life, and they shall never perish; neither shall anyone snatch them out of My hand.*

The most effective way to become victorious in spirituality is through faith (Hebrews 11:6) and to be led by God in accomplishing His will through His Word and the Holy Spirit, just as Jesus did during His time. The scriptures say He pleased God, was full of faith and wisdom, obeyed His Word and will, and endured the Cross (Hebrews 5:7-9) for our reconciliation. Christ would;

✓ Be consistent in His daily prayers and devotion to the Scriptures.
✓ Pursue and do God's will (John 14:30-31).
✓ Apply the Scriptures in the right way (Matthew 4:3-10) by living by and applying God's Word in all situations ("the Word alive in you").

✓ Understand His calling, purpose, and what He should accomplish.
✓ Be a life changer by transforming people's lives through love. He was anointed by the Holy Spirit and had faith to "move mountains." He taught, delivered, and healed those oppressed by the devil (Acts 10:38).
✓ Endure the trials and temptations that He encountered (Luke 22:28).
✓ Above all, He sacrificed Himself for our reconciliation with God through love.

c) Our growth can be gradual over a long period

One important point is that Christ had to grow spiritually from childhood until He began His ministry, which He achieved by embracing a life of prayer and sanctification (Luke 2:40). He was able to endure all His temptations and trials because He maintained the "oil" of regular devotion (Matthew 25:1-13).

> ▪ *If we are to overcome the devil, we have to strategically wage war with him while growing spiritually day by day.*

Although the ten virgins initially received the grace to walk in the light of true faith, they overlooked the need for spiritual growth. Because of the darkness of the night and temptation, the enemy then devised strategies to make them weary and "sleep" away from the light of true faith. All ten virgins eventually succumbed to the test. However, the five wise virgins managed to reconcile because they had not forsaken the oil of regular prayer.

To overcome the enemy, believers need strong faith and effective prayer. They should also aim to grow spiritually daily (2 Corinthians 4:13-18).

How do we wage war with the enemy?

Believers engage in spiritual warfare to turn curses into blessings by God's grace. Their faith and diligence will make blessings and breakthroughs manifest in their lives. God's blessings include spiritual growth, fruitfulness, achievements, good health, and protection.

Ephesians 6:10-19 teaches us how to resist and overcome the devil's forces of darkness with spiritual weapons. He aims to hinder blessings and salvation in our lives. Therefore:

- **Be courageous** and positive, looking up to God while being steadfast in your faith, regardless of tempestuous winds or circumstances (Ephesians 6:10; 1 Corinthians 15:58; 16:13-14).
- **The Word of God must be "alive in you."**
  John 8:31-32 Then Jesus said to those Jews who believed Him, "If you abide in My word, you are My disciples indeed. 32 And you shall know the truth, and the truth shall make you free.
  (John 15:7-8)
  You should understand the truth through the Word of God to avoid falling into sin when faced with temptation. You will reference the Word for any encounter or situation as you walk in it by faith. Engage in regular devotion to God's Word. Abiding in His Word pleases Him so much that you will obtain His favor, and He will fight for you in your battles.

- **Put on love, faith, and hope** (1 Thessalonians 5:8). Love pacifies a multitude of sins (1 Peter 4:8).
- **Cast down bad thoughts before they capture your mind.**
  2 Corinthians 10:4-5 For the weapons of our warfare are not carnal but mighty in God for pulling down strongholds, 5 casting down arguments and every high thing that exalts itself against the knowledge of God, bringing every thought into captivity to the obedience of Christ.
- **Hold on to the truth of the Word with steadfastness because you fear sinning against God.**
  Proverbs 16:6 In mercy and truth Atonement is provided for iniquity; And by the fear of the LORD one departs from evil.
  Be steadfast in resisting temptations from the enemy.
  (1 Peter 5:9)
- **Regularly conduct self-introspection to determine whether you are growing spiritually.**
  Assess your weaknesses and how the enemy is weakening or attacking your faith (2 Cor. 13:5).
  2 Corinthians 2:11 lest Satan should take advantage of us; for we are not ignorant of his devices.
- **Put on the whole armor of God** (Ephesians 6:11).

This implies standing steadfast in faith, praying, and "burning" with the light of good works as you grow in knowledge and spiritual understanding of the Word. This is for your fruitfulness as you look to Jesus. This involves the following key points:

- Ensure truthfulness.
- Embrace righteousness by ensuring your right standing with God.

- "Shod" yourself by preparing the gospel of peace and conveying the light of the gospel and its goodness in an inspiring manner.
- Use the shield of your faith to speak to and "move" your mountain or challenge in Jesus' name.
- Get hold of the Word. Do not lean on your own understanding.
- Interceding and praying in the Spirit. Through the power of words, you can break every yoke of the enemy, pull down strongholds, and dissolve various "hidden" or "subtle" spiritual attacks.

Most people with the world and its excitement at heart usually pray with the wrong motives. On the contrary, a believer will rejoice in the Lord rather than the world (Philippians 4:4). As long as we keep this in mind, we gain the strength to live out our prayer lives effectively since the prayer room is where we arm ourselves for victory in battle.

CHAPTER 4

FOUR CRUCIAL STRATEGIES TO CONQUER ANY SPIRITUAL BATTLE

This chapter will explore the key ways to overcome spiritual warfare and fight the enemy.

As mentioned before, a life of effective prayer and sanctification eventually leads to spiritual maturity. This is essential to magnify and impact the light of the gospel of salvation in people's lives (Matthew 5:16), for their conviction, conversion to faith, repentance, deliverance, and so on. The devil tries to suppress or hinder the shining of the gospel light, particularly among those believers who impart and share this light with others.

The journey of faith in Christ requires us to press on and resist the wiles and devices of the enemy as he tries to divert our paths from true faith.

The first thing to know about spiritual warfare is that believers are **overcomers** through Christ.

> *1 John 5:4 For whatever is born of God overcomes the world. And this is the victory that has overcome the world-our faith.*

A believer's ongoing warfare with the adversary, the devil, becomes a reality the moment they experience new birth.

By enlightening Christians through the gospel, the Word deposited in their hearts can elevate their spirituality more than ever before. A breakthrough like this is what the enemy resists the most.

Spiritual warfare is mainly centered on spiritual progress, growth, and breakthroughs in livelihood upkeep through faith in Christ, devotion, and obedience to the Word.

Our Race is a Battle

> *2 Corinthians 1:8 For we do not want you to be ignorant, brethren, of our trouble which came to us in Asia: that we were burdened beyond measure, above strength, so that we despaired even of life.*

In most physical confrontations or competitions like combat sports, strength and stamina are necessary to add to your skill. Otherwise, having only the skill will make you more vulnerable to your more agile but less skilled opponent.

Likewise, in the faith, you need the strength and stamina of mental endurance. To overcome, you must possess the character traits of being steadfast, positive, courageous, and always relying on and trusting in God, regardless of how tough it gets. Most people who are zealous for God endure hardships more than ordinary people because they continuously look to God. Such a rooted character will also aid in one's continuance in the Word and prayer as he learns obedience through walking in the Spirit.

This battle of resistance by the enemy starts in the mind. The devil uses all his subtle tricks and wiles to **divert** your focus from fulfilling and obeying the Word of God. He aims to replace the good intentions of the mind with carnal or fleshly deeds or a negative mentality. As a result, the enemy diverts the mind in various ways, including through bad influence, discouragement, enticement, contention, false religion, vain philosophy, pride, greed, and lust. This is such that a person ends up justifying himself or herself by doing actions or deeds contrary to the Word of God (Jeremiah 44:15-19).

The devil will influence the natural mindset of an individual so that he takes action contrary to pleasing God. This is because of a hardened conscience. The more a person is void of God's Word, the more vulnerable he is to losing the battle, especially when he faces trials or temptations. For us to safeguard ourselves in this spiritual battle, we need to emphasize the following key points:

Foundational Tips for Safeguarding Your Mind and Actions

- In any situation you encounter, be positive and focus on what the Word of God says rather than on the circumstances. Maintain a positive mindset and believe that "the dry bones will live," because with God, all things are possible.
- Your situation is not new; seek advice if possible and find out how other believers have managed to cross the same hurdle.
- Speak the Word of God to your situation and proclaim the name of Jesus. For instance, when facing family or personal

struggles, it is important to denounce every instance where the Word of God is being contradicted in your life. These include strife, hatred, infidelity, and drug abuse.

- Self-introspection: Be aware of the major areas where you are weaker or more vulnerable to falling easily. These are the "pressure points" that the enemy targets to strike without your awareness or through temptation.

- Do not touch or use the devil's "resources" for your benefit; otherwise, he will use them against you. It could be using corrupt shortcuts to gain favors or succeed, lying to get out of trouble, spreading gossip to manipulate situations, and more.

The Battle Requires Us to be Spiritually Equipped

(the four essential life-transforming qualities)

A believer in Christ should effectively use and maximize his faith as a mountain mover. God desires Christians to overcome this world as conquerors and life changers through the Holy Spirit. Believers share the light of the gospel with the world through the power and work of the Holy Spirit. People need to witness this light of virtue, through which believers can "move mountains" and transform lives. This transformation may take various forms, including miraculous healing, deliverance from oppression, or providing essential needs. This is so that people may believe and see the light of the gospel.

The following four qualities are necessary for a believer to progress in realizing and fulfilling God's plan for his life and witnessing the manifestation and life-transforming power of the Holy Spirit:

- ❖ Sanctification to holiness
- ❖ Application and revelation of the Word
- ❖ Abundant faith (speaking to your mountain)
- ❖ Endurance

With these four essential components, a believer will effect change in life situations and the world in the name of Jesus. They can also illuminate the gospel to the world, thus transforming people's lives and inspiring them to follow Christ and His Word (Acts 2:37). These qualities signify the ability to stand firm in faith and pursue eternal life. Believers become spiritually enriched by embracing these four essential qualities.

This leads to the following key factors:

A person is considered "spiritually rich" if they:

- ✓ Put the Word of God into practice in their daily lives (the Word "Alive in You")—thus, they become "living stones." (1 Peter 2:5).
- ✓ Are sanctified by the Holy Spirit (Christ abiding in them),
- ✓ Possess the power in Christ to move mountains (situations) by faith and utterance in the name of Jesus.

We may now look at these four qualities:

1. SANCTIFICATION TO HOLINESS

Being Separate and Set Apart

As discussed in the earlier chapters, sanctification, that is, the work of the Holy Spirit and His Word in purifying our hearts as we progress firmly in the faith, according to Ephesians 5:26-27,9-10, is a critical requirement. We need to grow spiritually to bear more fruit in holiness (keeping in mind that sanctification is also holiness). The heroes of faith in the Bible (Hebrews 11) were not only faithful to God, but were a people separated from the world. They remained committed to worshiping Him despite facing adversity (Daniel 1:8, 6:10-16).

Daniel, because of a prayerful and "undefiled" life dedicated to God, endured and saw the mighty hand of God deliver him from all his trials and temptations. He became exemplary.

> **_Daniel 6:10_** *Now when Daniel knew that the writing was signed, he went home. And in his upper room, with his windows open toward Jerusalem, he knelt down on his knees three times that day, and prayed and gave thanks before his God, as was his custom since early days.*

The 'heroes of faith' endured the courageous fight of faith. Their victories primarily centered around:

1. Faith in God,
2. The desire for a heavenly kingdom (Hebrews 11:14-16, 35),
3. The deliverance of the children of Israel from their bondage and enslavement by the surrounding kingdoms, and
4. The Old Covenant (sacrifices and statutes).

They were a "separated" people who dedicated their lives to abstaining from the pollution of the world (or Gentiles) and instead pursued God's will.

We become a "separate" people through sanctification and avoiding the pollution of this world. This entails becoming a 'royal priesthood' through Christ in us so that He transforms us into the fullness of His image and likeness. This is through our faith, the

Word, and the power of the Spirit of Christ, and by living a prayerful life so that we all become heirs of God.

Improve Your Spirituality

Be continually and gradually improving in yielding the fruit of the Spirit (2 Peter 1:5-11). It's a check and balance here, where you consistently observe and note areas where you are lacking. As you discover what you can do to improve yourself, you also ask for insight from God in your prayers. This is an important phase in a believer's life.

We must equip ourselves to bear the fruit of the Holy Spirit continuously rather than just staying at the same level of faith. Your life must not stagnate. You will experience the blessings and manifest presence of God in your life. This includes the ability to confront the wiles, trials, and temptations that come as the enemy tries to resist your steadfastness in faith.

Just as Daniel opened his windows daily to pray facing Jerusalem (Daniel 6:10), may you also open your heart and focus on Jesus and the heavenly Jerusalem (Hebrews 12:22-24) since you are a stranger in this world.

2. REVELATION AND APPLICATION OF GOD'S WORD

John 15:7-8 If you abide in Me, and My words abide in you, you will ask what you desire, and it shall be done for you. 8 By this My Father is glorified, that you bear much fruit; so you will be My disciples.

Most of us occasionally struggle to break through in life situations. This is primarily because we want to apply the Word of

God even when it is not "alive" in us. Obeying God's voice and Word is a lifestyle. After the Word has become alive in a Christian and mixed with his faith, it can be put into effect.

> ***Colossians 1:9-10*** *For this reason we also, since the day we heard it, do not cease to pray for you, and to ask that you may be filled with the knowledge of His will in all wisdom and spiritual understanding; 10 that you may walk worthy of the Lord, fully pleasing Him, being fruitful in every good work and increasing in the knowledge of God.*

From the above verses, we see two requisites:

a) Acquire knowledge of the Word to apply it to your specific situation.
b) Live the Word by obedience and bearing fruit ("the Word alive in you").

We can see this application and revelation of the Word of God when Daniel used his knowledge of the scriptures to realize that Israel's captivity had ended since the seventy years of their captivity had been fulfilled (Daniel 9:2).

It is through the knowledge of the Word that a person rises and takes steps. Daniel interceded by faith for Israel to return from captivity (Daniel 9:3-19). He did not separate himself from Israel's sin, but he humbled himself to become an intercessor and a mediator for Israel. Throughout all the fiery trials with his friends, his humility, obedience, and faith in God's covenant with Israel were evidence that the Word of God's covenant was alive in him. He believed in God's deliverance. As a result, God answered his prayer.

Moreover, a revelation gives us the knowledge and understanding needed to apply God's Word in specific situations. These steps enable God to open closed doors in our lives. Wisdom and knowledge are key. Without a sound knowledge of the Scriptures, Daniel might not have made such a fruitful prayer for the restoration of the children of Israel from captivity.

What is the Word of God saying about your situation?

✓ Are you supposed to repent of anything you have done wrong? Daniel took steps of humility and repentance by interceding for Israel's idolatry, which had caused them to fall into captivity.
✓ Should you destroy an idol or sin in your life?
✓ Have you forgiven those who have hurt you? Are you practicing love, especially toward your adversaries or those who do not wish you well?
✓ Are you allowing the Holy Spirit to lead and direct your ways?
✓ If in ministry, are you an intercessor? Are you carrying the right vision for your church according to God's plan or will for your life?
✓ If you need finances, do you ever consider how you can help someone in need or direct your help towards them, or are you thinking narrowly?

Have a revelation of what the Word of God is saying to you concerning your particular situation, and move and live according to the Word. It is through enlightenment and the Word that you have discernment or can judge circumstances. This way, you will be able to make the right decisions or take the correct steps as the Holy Spirit leads you.

Note: Seek guidance or advice from experienced, faithful, and godly people in the Body of Christ who have overcome similar life hurdles.

We also see that Joshua was instructed to meditate on the Word of God to become victorious in battle and occupy the Promised Land (Joshua 1:8-9). He obeyed and achieved success (Joshua 11:23).

Paul knew from the scriptures and by revelation (Colossians 1:25-29) that the gospel was for both Jews and Gentiles. The apostles reached out to the Gentiles through revelation, and the Word was alive in them. Even though trials, tribulations, and persecution pressed them on all sides, they still preached and spread the gospel. They endured because the Word was alive in them.

> *<u>1 Thessalonians 2:1-6</u> For you yourselves know, brethren, that our coming to you was not in vain. 2 But even after we had suffered before and were spitefully treated at Philippi, as you know, we were bold in our God to speak to you the gospel of God in much conflict. 3 For our exhortation did not come from error or uncleanness, nor was it in deceit. 4 But as we have been approved by God to be entrusted with the gospel, even so we speak, not as pleasing men, but God who tests our hearts. 5 For neither at any time did we use flattering words, as you know, nor a cloak for covetousness — God is witness. 6 Nor did we seek glory from men, either from you or from others, when we might have made demands as apostles of Christ.*
>
> *10 You are witnesses, and God also, how devoutly and justly and blamelessly we behaved ourselves among you who believe; 11 as you know how we exhorted, and comforted, and charged every*

one of you, as a father does his children, 12 that you would walk
worthy of God who calls you into His own kingdom and glory.

During the time of the prophets (1 Kings 22:29-37), King Ahab knew that Ramoth-Gilead, a city seized and colonized by the Syrians, belonged to them. He was confident he could go to war to recover it. Hence, he requested King Jehoshaphat to ally with him. However, King Ahab was an idolatrous king of Israel who did not observe God's statutes. This implied that the Word of God was not "alive" in him. Because of this, he failed to regain the city, lost the war, and was killed.

Remember the sons of Sceva, who failed to cast out an evil spirit because the Word of the gospel was not alive in them, though they knew that Paul was mightily used by God (Acts 19:13-16). Thus, we are called to become "living stones" (1 Peter 2:5), in the sense that the Word of the gospel is alive in us, that is, "living" the Word.

3. OUR FAITH

Speak to Your Mountain or Situation

Our faith is one of the most effective weapons in spiritual warfare. Simply put, faith in God is being free of doubt whenever you look up to and rely on God.

Through the Holy Spirit, our faith, and the revelation of the gospel's Word, Christ has given us the power to speak to our situations and change them in His name. As long as you are in Christ, you are already at that high spiritual level of power to move mountains by faith because Christ said it Himself (Luke 10:19-20).

> *__Mark 11:22-23__ So Jesus answered and said to them, "Have faith in God. 23 For assuredly, I say to you, whoever says to this mountain, 'Be removed and be cast into the sea,' and does not doubt in his heart, but believes that those things he says will be done, he will have whatever he says.*
>
> *...26 But if you do not forgive, neither will your Father in heaven forgive your trespasses."*

It is now just a matter of exercising your faith and speaking to your situation. Let us remember that God's creation was through the spoken Word (Hebrews 11:3).

> *__Numbers 20:7-8__ Then the Lord spoke to Moses, saying, 8 "Take the rod; you and your brother Aaron gather the congregation together. Speak to the rock before their eyes, and it will yield its water; thus you shall bring water for them out of the rock, and give drink to the congregation and their animals."*

God instructed Moses to speak to the rock as they journeyed to the Promised Land because of their dire need for water. We have also been given the same command. God has called all believers to speak to the Rock that is high above in prayer and true faith (Jeremiah 33:3). He will give them living water (His Spirit) and His Word, springing up into abundant life, and they will reach the Promised Land (John 7:38-39).

Because of the Israelites, Moses was distracted from speaking to the physical rock and failed to enter Canaan (Numbers 20:1-13). However, he served God and Israel faithfully. We can learn from Moses' experience that the rock was ready to respond to his command had he spoken a word instead of striking the rock with his staff. Likewise, God Himself and our situations are ready to respond to our spoken words of faith before we even attempt alternative steps or shortcuts.

Christ has given us the power to speak to our situations (in the name of Jesus) in our lives as we approach the "promised life." For this reason, we have confidence and faith that God will raise the standard in any restricted situation or narrow path ahead of us (Isaiah 59:19).

Through our faith, Christ has given us power and raised us up in the spiritual realm.

> _**Ephesians 2:4-7**_ _But God, who is rich in mercy, because of His great love with which He loved us, 5 even when we were dead in trespasses, made us alive together with Christ (by grace you have been saved), 6 and raised us up together, and made us sit together in the heavenly places in Christ Jesus, 7 that in the ages to come He might show the exceeding riches of His grace in His kindness toward us in Christ Jesus._

The city of the Jebusites, today known as Jerusalem, was situated at a higher altitude than any other settlement. Because of this, the king of the Jebusites would easily defeat his enemies. This was done by simply rolling stones downhill to crush them using the least powerful of his minions or his weakest servants, such as the blind, the lame, and the poor men. For this reason, King David desired it and eventually seized it from the king of the Jebusites.

> _**2 Samuel 5:6-8**_ _And the king and his men went to Jerusalem against the Jebusites, the inhabitants of the land, who spoke to David, saying, "You shall not come in here; but the blind and the lame will repel you," thinking, "David cannot come in here." 7_

> *Nevertheless David took the stronghold of Zion (that is, the City of David). 8 Now David said on that day, "Whoever climbs up by way of the water shaft and defeats the Jebusites (the lame and the blind, who are hated by David's soul), he shall be chief and captain."...*

Similarly, Christ has elevated us to a higher spiritual realm by giving us the power to exercise our faith and "bind" the enemy's schemes and devices. This is through the power of faith in Him and the Word of the gospel (Ephesians 2:6).

> *<u>Matthew 16:19</u> "And I will give you the keys of the kingdom of heaven, and whatever you bind on earth will be bound in heaven, and whatever you loose on earth will be loosed in heaven."*

(Matthew 17:20).

Even the weakest of the saints can achieve great things through faith and the Holy Spirit, just like the blind and the Jebusites defeated King David at first. King David had to climb through a tunnel and go through a shaft with his army to eventually defeat the Jebusites and occupy Jerusalem (2 Samuel 5:8). Thus, even the weakest of saints can dismantle and dissolve the schemes or devices of the forces of evil that oppose us because of the power of the Holy Spirit through faith in Christ.

- *As long as a person is in the truth of faith, he is fighting from a higher spiritual realm than the forces of darkness.*

This is because:

> *<u>Zechariah 4:6b:</u> 'Not by might nor by power, but by My Spirit.'*

Christ has raised us to this new life of faith through our knowledge of Him and the **revelation** of His Word through the gospel. Being raised high above implies that believers can move mountains and dissolve challenges in life by exercising their faith as kings and priests (Revelation 5:10).

Speak to your problem and proclaim the Word that relates to your situation, especially when you are confident that the Word of God is "alive and powerful" to overcome any challenge. God will give you wisdom and the power to overcome or overthrow your "mountain," even when it seems otherwise, just as He did for King David (2 Samuel 5:8). The enemy had a huge advantage, to the extent that he used only the blind and lame to overthrow King David and other rivals. However, his dominance did not last long because God helped King David and his army discover and strategically climb through a tunnel. They rose up, overthrew the Jebusites, and conquered the city.

Therefore, be prayerful and commit your situation to God. The Holy Spirit will direct you to your "source" of breakthrough or turning point. He will grant you the wisdom and power to overcome your situation.

4. ENDURANCE

> _**2 Timothy 2:1**_ _You therefore, my son, be strong in the grace that is in Christ Jesus._
>
> _**verse 3**_ _You therefore must endure hardship as a good soldier of Jesus Christ._

Hebrews 11 gives examples of many distinguished men and women who became victors, or "heroes," because of their faith, obedience, and reliance on God to overcome their battles. They also caused a tremendous impact by delivering the traditional church (the twelve tribes) from their surrounding enemies by the hand of God during their time (the old covenant).

It was not an easy battle, as they faced much opposition (Hebrews 11:33-40). Moses encountered much resistance from the children of Israel because of their unbelief. During the prophets' era, there was so much idolatry and resistance to God's covenant that the children of Israel persecuted and killed their prophets and the people of God (Matthew 23:37).

Christ highlighted that believers would suffer for the gospel (Mark 13:13; Philippians 1:29). The simple reason is this: they are a threat to the enemy. Their faith in Christ and holiness will change the enemy's course and overthrow his schemes. For this reason, the Bible states that we are more than conquerors, even in the face of persecution, tribulation, or death.

> *__Romans 8:35,37__ Who shall separate us from the love of Christ? Shall tribulation, or distress, or persecution, or famine, or nakedness, or peril, or sword?*
>
> *37 Yet in all these things we are more than conquerors through Him who loved us.*

The devil persecutes believers because he realizes their richness—they possess faith, knowledge of the Word, and the pursuit of holiness. Through Christ, believers have the ability and power to suppress the enemy and overthrow his devices. It is not only about changing life situations, but also becoming a shining light to others and transforming their lives. This is through the illumination of the gospel, to pull others out of bondage and captivity and to declare blessings instead of curses, so that we may all be joined in the unity of faith.

> *Jude 22-23 And on some have compassion, making a distinction; 23 but others save with fear, pulling them out of the fire, hating even the garment defiled by the flesh.*

The "richer" we are spiritually, that is, being sanctified in holiness and having the ability to apply God's Word (by revelation and faith) to reverse and triumph over the enemy's devices, the more we shine as "lights." The more we become life changers in the world, the more we are a threat to the enemy.

Moreover, it does not always follow that believers who are rich in faith will not face trials or persecution. The opposite is true because this journey or race of faith is a spiritual battle.

(2 Thessalonians 1:3-5; 1 Peter 5:8-10; Hebrews 11:33-39).

Thus, believers should endure trials, persevere, and resist temptations by being steadfast in their faith and good deeds. Because of their unwavering faith, they will gain the experience to know how to handle life situations wisely (James 1:2-4). As a result, they are molded and transformed to develop a good character endowed with knowledge and trust in God. God will help them overcome to deserve the crown of life.

CHAPTER 5

TEN ESSENTIAL COMPONENTS FOR BUILDING A POWERFUL CHURCH

To achieve effective functionality and spiritual growth within the Body of Christ

This chapter discusses the vital components of faith that the church must wholeheartedly uphold under God's guidance and protection. Believers must always seek God's guidance. They should be guided by the Holy Spirit so that the church can function effectively and be a light to the world. Believers glorify God as they unite in faith and support each other's spiritual growth in holiness through abundant grace.

The Function of the Church

The core mission and purpose of the Body of Christ, the church, is to equip believers with the gospel, edify, and help people grow spiritually (Ephesians 4:11-13) while glorifying God. It is through the washing and cleansing by the Word in holiness that Christ receives to Himself a glorious church for eternal glory (Ephesians 5:26-27).

Each member of the Body has a unique and individual role in maintaining this function through the unity of faith and fellowship (Ephesians 4:16). In addition, the church must convey the gospel to the world in love so that people may also receive the grace and gift of salvation through Jesus Christ.

Christ's Commandment to the Church

Christ desires and instructs the church to:

- **Show love** in the Body of Christ and the world (John 13:34; 1 Thessalonians 3:12-13).
- **Live a truthful life** so that your light shines as you become an impactful and influential person who leads by example for God's glory (Matthew 5:16). This entails pursuing godliness and avoiding evil.
- Become **profitable** by spreading the gospel, winning souls, making disciples, and bearing fruit through the Word (John 15:16).
- **Edify** and **equip** believers to **serve God** and **grow spiritually** through different ministry disciplines (Ephesians 4:16).
- Continue magnifying and **glorifying God**; stay connected in fellowship and ministry by offering the sacrifices of prayer, worship, and praise to Him like burning incense (Revelation 5:8).

Christ's Prayer for the Disciples and the Church

Did you know that Christ's prayer for His disciples and the church at the Last Supper had a tremendous impact on the early church? This was so much that, in such a short period, the disciples converted to the faith in multitudes. The apostles performed many signs, miracles, and wonders. The disciples continued in one accord through prayer and sharing the Word of God (Acts 2:46-47).

This rapid growth of the early church, along with their love for one another and zeal for God, will always be remembered. How much more, in this day and age, will it be for those who believe, if they continue in prayer and intercession for the modern-day church?

The following are some of the prayer points made by the Lord Christ as He prayed for His disciples and the church in John Chapter 17:

- That Christ may be glorified in the church (verse 1).
- That they may know the only true God (verse 3).
- To be kept in oneness and unity in the faith of the gospel (verse 11).
- To be kept from evil (verse 15).
- To be sanctified through the Word of God (verse 17).
- To become heirs of His eternal glory (verse 24).
- That the world may be able to see the glorious light of the church for the glory of God (verse 23).
- That He may dwell in them for their spiritual soundness in the unity of faith as one Body in Christ (verse 23).

To follow Christ's example, we need to pray for the church regularly, focusing on the points mentioned above and other crucial requests.

We need to offer such prayers constantly to empower ourselves spiritually. This will strengthen our faith, both individually and collectively as the Body of the church, for its growth in Christ. Besides attributes of spiritual growth such as knowledge, wisdom, and faith that I have discussed previously, other important aspects of prayer can equip members of the Body of Christ to function effectively.

Serving and Edifying One Another in Love

> *John 13:34-35 A new commandment I give to you, that you love one another; as I have loved you, that you also love one another. 35 By this all will know that you are My disciples, if you have love for one another.*

The foundation of the faith is Christ, and for Him to work in believers to cleanse them through the Word of God to present to Himself a glorious and holy church (Ephesians 5:26-27), for eternal glory. For this reason, believers are called to serve and edify one another through love.

> *1 Thessalonians 3:12-13 And may the Lord make you increase and abound in love to one another and to all, just as we do to you, 13 so that He may establish your hearts blameless in holiness before our God and Father at the coming of our Lord Jesus Christ with all His saints.*

This is because we are members of one another. When we pray for unbelievers, our main concern is to pray for their illumination so that the light of the gospel of Christ may shine in their hearts. (2 Corinthians 4:3-5).

Besides loving one another, we must shine as lights to become a living testimony to unbelievers. This is so that the gospel and our good deeds will illuminate their hearts and strengthen their resolve to follow Christ through conviction and repentance.

10 STRATEGIES FOR COMBATING SPIRITUAL WARFARE

The following 10 strategies, or virtues, make believers' prayers effective (both corporate and individual):

❖ *Press Forward to Cause an Impact*

Christians should strive to strengthen their faith to positively impact the lives of others so that the name of God is glorified.

> *Mark 2:1-12*
>
> *3 Then they came to Him, bringing a paralytic who was carried by four men. 4 And when they could not come near Him because of the crowd, they uncovered the roof where He was. So when they had broken through, they let down the bed on which the paralytic was lying. 5 When Jesus saw their faith, He said to the paralytic, "Son, your sins are forgiven you."*
>
> *...11 "I say to you, arise, take up your bed, and go to your house." 12 Immediately he arose, took up the bed, and went out in the presence of them all, so that all were amazed and glorified God, saying, "We never saw anything like this!"*

According to scripture, Christ healed the paralyzed man because of the faith of others rather than his own. The four men who bore his bed had so much faith that they stretched the scope of their minds to do the unexpected—opening the rooftop—to the extent that his sinful life was blotted out (verse 5). Thus, the paralyzed man was made whole, not only physically, but also because his sins were forgiven, his spiritual life was restored, and he believed in Christ.

If we raise the standard of our faith today, without looking back, God can work miraculous wonders (Mark 11:22-24). Through the power of faith, God will respond to our prayers of intercession for our neighbors and loved ones. Because of virtue and faith in believers, they can be healed and converted to the gospel faith for the glory of God. When we see these things happening, we become more motivated to continue pressing forward, even as we encounter life's challenges.

❖ *Intercession by Abundant Faith*

Is your country, church, or close family in urgent need of spiritual healing? We can resolve this issue using the story I discussed in Mark 2:1-12. For deliverance to manifest in any people, nation, or situation, there will always be a need for people who:

- ✓ Will raise a standard of faith to the extent that they also:
- ✓ Make a further step of rising to be seen, that is, letting that light of faith become visible by standing up for their faith, and then,
- ✓ Use a Word in season to convey the ailment to the Lord Jesus.
- ✓ Be influential and guide others to follow God's plan. For example, the prophets in the Old Testament tried to refrain the Israelites from worshiping idols so that they would obey God's statutes (Matthew 23:37-39).

It does not necessarily need a "prominent prophet" or "popular man of God," so to speak, because these four men were ordinary individuals. It might just require a few individuals from within a community who arise because of their high level of faith. Because of such faith, we, the people or congregation of the general or ordinary faith, will observe them evidently stretching themselves to stand in a position of seeking God's hand, to the point where they then direct the ailment to Christ's feet. In any society, and by His mercy, God desires to raise men of faith who can speak His message (Word in season) and inspire people to follow His guidance.

This is what those four men did (Mark 2:1-12). They raised their standard of faith, became bold enough to rise above the ordinary level of life to go up to the rooftop (the life of walking in the light), and then directed the ailment to the Lord Himself (looking to Jesus, Hebrews 12:2).

One of the key fundamentals of effective prayer is intercession, which requires raising our faith standard. This is one of the key things the Old Testament teaches us. God sent people from different backgrounds, such as shepherds, scribes, and exiled captives, to become intercessors for the children of Israel with the hope of their restoration, that is, Israel's repentance to obey the Covenant of Statutes. The goal was to break free from their oppression due to the surrounding Gentile nations. One example is Daniel's intercession for the children of Israel. His humility, peculiarity, and faith made a huge impact.

These men had to:

(1) Raise their faith standard.

(2) Become visible by standing in a position of ministry or stepping out of an ordinary lifestyle to become peculiar (conducting ministry and prophesying the spiritual oracles of God).

(3) Direct or petition the captivity into the hands of the Lord God, especially through sacrificial prayer and intercession.

(4) Deliver God's Word in season and guide the people according to God's plan. They emphasized the need for rectification and reconciliation, and encouraged people to follow God's purpose and Word.

Thus, it is important to stand out and exercise a high level of faith, just as the prophets of old did. They were evidently peculiar compared to the general populace for this type of intercession. This is because of their extraordinary faith (Daniel 3:16-18). The Lord Jesus Christ Himself, in the days of His flesh and His ministry of the gospel, was full of faith. He became visibly and evidently peculiar because He interceded and worked deliverance for the Jews by moving in faith and obeying God's Word.

Note: The Church can be deprived of men of influence and faith because of the enemy, who attempts to replace them with false teachers who, through deception, lead people astray (Acts 20:28-31; 2 Corinthians 11:12-15). This is a major form of spiritual warfare; it should be a key prayer point in the Church.

❖ *Being Zealous for the Things of God*

The one thing we know is the zeal of the early church in Jerusalem during the days of the twelve apostles. Their ministry was based on willingness and love for one another. They showed love and support to each other, shared provisions, and continued in daily assembly prayers regardless of facing persecution. They moved in the power of the Holy Spirit and the doctrine of Christ.

Even though the early church had limited revelation to spread the gospel to the Gentiles, God eventually provided this illumination through the apostle Paul (Galatians 2:9; Ephesians 3:3-9; Acts 15). When we are zealous for God's things, God strengthens us, enlightens us, and gives us the wisdom to move on the right path in the faith journey.

In modern-day life, we also need that zeal to keep the fire of the Word of the gospel burning in our hearts. This is so that we do not faint, do God's work without wholeheartedness, or draw backward in times of need.

> *Revelation 2:4-5* (to the church in Ephesus);
> *4 Nevertheless I have this against you, that you have left your first love. 5 Remember therefore from where you have fallen; repent and do the first works, or else I will come to you quickly and remove your lampstand from its place — unless you repent.*

To minister to others, a believer should always have a positive mindset of laboring in love. The more zealous we are, the more God uses us to function effectively in the Body of Christ as we serve fellow members according to our abilities.

❖ *Humility*

Humility is rooted in dying to self to submit to God's will by abiding in His Word. Rather than just being an attitude or mindset, it is a personality issue of the inner man. Having the right attitude helps a lot as one of the first steps in growing in humility, as we see in the following verses:

> *__Mark 9:35__ And He sat down, called the twelve, and said to them, "If anyone desires to be first, he shall be last of all and servant of all".*

> *__Romans 12:3__ For I say, through the grace given to me, to everyone who is among you, not to think of himself more highly than he ought to think, but to think soberly, as God has dealt to each one a measure of faith.*

Humility is the ability to yield and submit to God, individuals of higher status, and all people through a mentality of modesty without pride or feeling superior. It involves possessing modesty, meekness, and lowliness of the heart. This mindset places God's will first with goodness and gentleness (Romans 12:16). A humble person avoids the mentality or notion that one's success is because of his own will and power without acknowledging and giving glory to God.

It entails basing one's progress on God's grace and power and avoiding self-elevation. One can do this by constantly referring to the Word of God rather than one's own perspective in any situation. Therefore, humility makes us serve one another in love without focusing on ourselves but on the needs of others, according to God's will.

Attributes of Humility

— It leads to a personality of godly contentment (Philippians 4:11-13) and esteeming others better than oneself (Philippians 2:2-4). Humility implies accepting one's errors, embracing corrections, and yielding to God's Word. Reconciliation with God begins with peacefully reconciling sour relationships through forgiveness (Matthew 5:23-25).

It allows people to treat others with respect, kindness, and understanding. Humble people make peace.

— A humble person boldly exposes sin whenever necessary to warn others without feeling ashamed, and to please God.

— A humble person submits to God's plan, which might differ greatly from their personal goals or ambitions. They submit to others.

— They serve, help, and uplift others. Thus, they show love through cheerful giving, ministering, and other means of uplifting others.

— Humility attracts answered prayers and spiritual excellence, as well as blessings and breakthroughs (1 Peter 5:6-7). Christians can create a good atmosphere for divine favor and protection by not seeking personal glory, but giving glory to God.

— They are content and thankful, especially to God, for what they have attained or received (Philippians 4:11-13).

The story of Naaman the leper teaches us how humility eventually leads to a blessing from God.

2 Kings 5:12b-14

...So he turned and went away in a rage. 13 And his servants came near and spoke to him, and said, "My father, if the prophet had told you to do something great, would you not have done it? How much more then, when he says to you, 'Wash, and be clean'?" 14 So he went down and dipped seven times in the Jordan, according to the saying of the man of God; and his flesh was restored like the flesh of a little child, and he was clean.

Naaman would have missed his breakthrough in healing if he had not been humble enough to dip himself into the "unfavorable" river Jordan.

We are called to "dip" ourselves into a life of serving, helping, and positively impacting others through the gospel, financial support, or life skills. Our ambition should extend beyond merely improving ourselves and our families (or just those "clean and smooth" flowing rivers).

May you serve God in humility, and then He will gladly prosper you in all your endeavors. This was the case with Naaman, whom God restored to health. Let us allow God to use us in His kingdom for His glory rather than for our personal ambitions or vain desires.

Humility implies submitting to God in every aspect of life and confessing our sins. The contrite spirit of sincere remorse is filled with guilt and a desire for atonement. This yields a desire for reconciliation with God whenever we err or fall short in our walk of faith. It allows Him to direct our steps because He will surely guide us.

> **Psalms 25:9** *The humble He guides in justice, And the humble He teaches His Way.*
>
> **Psalms 34:18** *The Lord is near to those who have a broken heart, And saves such as have a contrite spirit.*

❖ *Coming Boldly to the Throne of Grace*
Confession

1 John 1:9 If we confess our sins, He is faithful and just to forgive us our sins and to cleanse us from all unrighteousness.

God is love, and He is always ready to cleanse us from all unrighteousness. Whenever we fall into error, we should confidently repent and pour our hearts out to God before taking any steps of faith or engaging in our daily activities. Reconciliation is the key to progressive steps.

Make it a regular practice to cast your worries to God, especially your flaws, so that He can correct you. Whenever we pray, we should examine ourselves first and confess our errors so that we are free from guilt or the burden of our past mistakes.

That we remain faithful in times of trial or challenge

The Bible gives us many instances of people who remained faithful to God in the face of difficulties and persecution. Joseph is a good example. He did not hold grudges against his brothers, regardless of their malicious treatment. He remained faithful to Potiphar's household by rejecting his wife (Genesis 39:8-10).

Daniel and his friends refused to worship idols even after being threatened with the death penalty (Daniel 3). We also need God to strengthen and comfort us so that we remain faithful to withstand such strongholds that oppose God's will.

Pursuing peace

Romans 12:18 If it is possible, as much as depends on you, live peaceably with all men.

Always pray for wisdom, seek peace with everyone, and be penitent before God. In this way, it becomes easier to continue in prayer peacefully, with minimal mental discouragement or strain that we often experience. It is crucial to release grudges from our hearts so that we do not fall into condemnation (James 5:9).

When we pursue peace with others, we dissolve psychological tensions. The ability to amicably solve problems such as family disputes, financial contentions, the backsliding of fellow believers, and social issues helps us to become stronger and endure in our faith. God acts on our faith. The more we forgive or become at peace with one another, the more we will see His hand in blessings and answered prayers (Mark 11:25-26; Matthew 18:32-35).

A forgiving heart allows a believer's prayers to have a great impact through faith.

❖ *Guidance of the Holy Spirit*

> **<u>Romans 8:5-6</u>** *For those who live according to the flesh set their minds on the things of the flesh, but those who live according to the Spirit, the things of the Spirit. 6 For to be carnally minded is death, but to be spiritually minded is life and peace.*

If we desire guidance from the Holy Spirit, we must submit to Him. Praying that we don't follow, be influenced by, or be driven by the carnal or worldly mindset is an essential first step. Having a spiritual perspective is important to counteract and balance out a worldly mindset that spends much time and focuses on worldly goals and pursuits. This limits the time for regular prayer and devotional Bible study.

We must have a **spiritually sensitive** inner man so that we can discern the circumstances around us, or even hear God's voice, so that we know what to do and what path to take.

> *Romans 8:14* *For as many as are led by the Spirit of God, these are sons of God.*

The Holy Spirit shows us the path, directs us towards proper life goals, and reveals our individual calling in the service or ministry of the gospel. He strengthens us spiritually and physically whenever we become weak in adversity or temptation.

The Holy Spirit strengthens us to continue in obedience even when we cannot see the light or positivity in the work of ministry or our life struggles, ventures, or aspirations. He also enlightens and teaches us God's Word (John 14:26).

Therefore, we should:

1. Yield,
2. Learn from Him,
3. Serve in the Body according to the ability that God gives through the work of the Holy Spirit.
   > *1 Peter 4:11* *If anyone speaks, let him speak as the oracles of God. If anyone ministers, let him do it as with the ability which God supplies, that in all things God may be glorified through Jesus Christ, to whom belong the glory and the dominion forever and ever. Amen.*

❖ *Seeking to Please God*

> *John 5:30 I can of Myself do nothing. As I hear, I judge; and My judgment is righteous, because I do not seek My own will but the will of the Father who sent Me.*

We must incline our hearts toward pursuing God's purpose and will more than our desires and ambitions. Whatever you do, do it for the glory of God (Colossians 3:17), as we serve Christ, whereto we are called. We should not try to fit God's plan into our own desires, but we should align our desires to fit into God's plan and will concerning our lives. Thus, we should purposefully serve God and one another for His glory with a cheerful heart.

❖ *Becoming Servants of Righteousness*

This entails yielding the fruit of righteous deeds in love. Believers should be thankful and acknowledge the grace of our Lord Jesus, who has delivered them from the power of darkness, so that they become servants of righteousness, as a gift from God (Romans 5:17; 6:18). Therefore, they must illuminate the world with the gospel through their good deeds.

> *Ephesians 5:8-11 For you were once darkness, but now you are light in the Lord. Walk as children of light 9 (for the fruit of the Spirit is in all goodness, righteousness, and truth), 10 finding out what is acceptable to the Lord. 11 And have no fellowship with the unfruitful works of darkness, but rather expose them.*

(Job 29:12-16; Matthew 5:16)

The pursuit of righteousness implies being spiritual and not only religious.

Being a servant of righteousness will entail the following qualities:

- ✓ Serving and doing God's work responsibly and willingly from the heart rather than just fulfilling obligations, duty schedules, or outward impressions.
- ✓ Commitment to serving God and fellow believers in love.
- ✓ Concern for the well-being and welfare of fellow believers, your neighbors or relatives, and others.
- ✓ Being generous, helping others, and attending to people in need whenever you can.
- ✓ Having compassion for the lost and interceding for them so that they may also obtain salvation.
- ✓ A genuine and sincere heart (repentance and the fear of God).
- ✓ Seeking to grow more in the knowledge of the Word of God.
- ✓ Having delight and enthusiasm in fellowship and serving in the Body of Christ (Psalms 122:1).
- ✓ Reverence and respect for those above you and everyone, while pursuing peace with people whenever possible.
- ✓ Effective personal and corporate 'Word' devotion and prayer.

❖ *Attending to the Needs of Others*

Romans 15:2 Let each of us please his neighbour for his good, leading to edification.

Notice the key word here is "edifying," which means to empower or uplift someone to a much higher spiritual level and personality than he was before.

The Body of Christ functions, or edifies, by each member pushing or supplying another for spiritual uplifting.

Ephesians 4:15-16 But, speaking the truth in love, may grow up in all things into Him who is the head – Christ – 16 from whom the whole body, joined and knit together by what every joint supplies, according to the effective working by which every part does its share, causes growth of the body for the edifying of itself in love.

A wise approach is to realize your calling or line of service and see it as a need for fellow believers. See yourself as a servant who is called to serve Christ through serving others in love, thus showing God's love (John 13:14-15) in various ways such as intercession, exhortation, teaching, counseling, provisions, charity work, and hospitality. Thus, members of the Body build each other up in the church so that all become spiritually equipped. This implies the growth of the inner man in every member of the Body. This is so that the church may be one in faith and the likeness of Christ.

To live out our faith, we should also pray for the ability to identify and meet other people's needs, whether they are material, emotional, spiritual, or physical.

❖ *Sharing the Good News of the Gospel*

<u>*Hebrews 6:10-11*</u> *For God is not unjust to forget your work and labour of love which you have shown toward His name, in that you have ministered to the saints, and do minister. 11 And we desire that each one of you show the same diligence to the full assurance of hope until the end.*

Let us not grow weary of conveying the gospel to the world and enlightening others whenever the door or platform is open. Continue exhorting, motivating, and serving others by showing the light of spiritual virtue and good deeds for their inspiration and upliftment.

I would like to imagine ministering to others in the way our Lord Jesus did. Christ expounded and revealed the Word in a way that was inspiring, helpful, and uplifting to people. He preached deliverance so extensively that the oppressed and despondent found hope and glorified God through him (Acts 10:38). He was also exemplary in His love for God and in seeking the lost.

As we can see in Hebrews 6:10, the brethren conveyed the message out of love. This was a labor of love. They were also diligent in the full assurance of hope, implying that they were watchful to continue moving in the gospel faith.

> **_Ephesians 6:15_** _and having shod your feet with the preparation of the gospel of peace._

To be shod with the gospel of peace, we must continually walk in faith and love. The apostle Paul urged us to follow him since he was also a true follower of Christ (1 Corinthians 11:1) and fought a courageous fight of faith.

Being shod and prepared with the gospel of peace means standing your ground steadfastly and stomping on the fallen enemy, just as Roman soldiers did in their battles. Use your faith and utterance by pronouncing the Word of Truth relating to your situation. Such utterance "dissolves" and "stomps" the enemy's devices and intentions, dispelling their influence.

Conveying the gospel often comes with resistance or persecution. Christ frequently warned His disciples to remain firm and wise (Matthew 10:16-20). We should persevere, abstain, and resist evil while adhering to the Word of the gospel, so that, when we proclaim the gospel, we glorify God's name.

❖ *That we do not look back or draw back*

> *Hebrews 10:38-39 Now the just shall live by faith; But if anyone draws back, My soul has no pleasure in him. 39 But we are not of those who draw back to perdition, but of those who believe to the saving of the soul.*

The Bible highlights that our salvation and victory is affirmed on the condition that:

> *Hebrews 3:14 For we have become partakers of Christ if we hold the beginning of our confidence steadfast to the end.*

In other words, we should continue pressing on as we see the day approaching.

> *Philippians 3:14-15 I press toward the goal for the prize of the upward call of God in Christ Jesus. 15 Therefore let us, as many as are mature, have this mind; and if in anything you think otherwise, God will reveal even this to you.*

The apostle Paul says he fought and kept the faith to the end (2 Timothy 4:7). Those who draw back or fall away along the way risk missing out on this great and precious promise.

> *Hebrews 4:1 Therefore, since a promise remains of entering His rest, let us fear lest any of you seem to have come short of it.*

This will be their fate unless they rise and get back into the course of the race (Hebrews 12:12-17), just as the five wise virgins did (Matthew 25:5).

Because modern life dynamics have diverted much of our focus away from Christ, many Christians are losing their zeal, passion, and energy for the gospel they originally started with. Why so? People often view the Christian faith as a traditional religion rather than a life in Christ. They also lack revelation of His eternal preeminence as the Author of salvation (Colossians 1:18).

As the day approaches, we must pursue the gospel as a "life in Christ" of drawing near to God. This affects our thinking and approach to faith in God by motivating us daily to continue running and pressing toward the goal.

For the ten points aforementioned to become effective, the church should uphold the following key pillars:

- Pray without ceasing.
- Stay in the Word and doctrine of Christ.
- Encourage personal Bible study and participation in ministerial activities to ensure the growth of believers.
- Engage in soul-winning and discipleship through sincere and credible leadership.

CONCLUSION

Let us continue to keep up with prayer and devotion so that we may strengthen our spirituality in all its facets through true faith in Christ. This way, we become victors, just like the heroes of faith in the old days. They were exemplary in their courage and determination. As a result, they took bold steps to overcome the troubles they encountered. This was to the extent that their prayers and testimony of the Word moved God's heart to act on their behalf. In the same way, God will raise a standard for you to climb your mountain, and you will not be moved, especially when you fight using prayer and the Word of God (Ephesians 6:17-18), to:

- Raise the standard of your personality through faith, love, sincerity, and the fear of God.
- Increase your knowledge of Word application to real-life situations.
- Speak to your mountain or situation by faith.
- Overcome spiritual battles by safeguarding yourself from worldly elements and the wiles of the enemy while walking cautiously.
- Ensure your election and calling through diligence to eternal salvation.

Above all, grow spiritually through the Word and prayer, in faith and hope in Christ, to fulfill your purpose and reach your destiny. Glory be to God and the Lord Jesus forevermore.

~AMEN~

Thanks for reading! If you enjoyed this book or found it useful, I'd be very grateful if you could leave me a short review on Amazon. Your support does make a difference. Thank you.

1. You can leave a review by scanning the QR code below with your camera to go directly to the review page.
2. Or, visit your Amazon Orders page, find this book, and click "Write a Product Review."

www.ingramcontent.com/pod-product-compliance
Lightning Source LLC
Chambersburg PA
CBHW020553030426
42337CB00013B/1073